INVESTING IN THE NATIONAL RESEARCH INITIATIVE

An Update of the
Competitive Grants Program of the
U.S. Department of Agriculture

Board on Agriculture

National Research Council

NATIONAL ACADEMY PRESS
Washington, D.C. 1994

NATIONAL ACADEMY PRESS • 2101 Constitution Avenue, N.W. • Washington, D.C. 20418

NOTICE: The project that is the subject of this report was approved by the Governing Board of the National Research Council, whose members are drawn from the councils of the National Academy of Sciences, the National Academy of Engineering, and the Institute of Medicine. The members of the committee responsible for the report were chosen for their special competencies and with regard for appropriate balance.

This report has been reviewed by a group other than the authors according to procedures approved by a Report Review Committee consisting of members of the National Academy of Sciences, the National Academy of Engineering, and the Institute of Medicine.

This study was supported by the Cooperative State Research Service of the U.S. Department of Agriculture, under Agreement No. 94-COOP-2-0001 and by the Farm Foundation, and the W. K. Kellogg Foundation. Additional support was provided by the National Research Council. Any opinions, findings, conclusions, or recommendations expressed in this publication are those of the Board on Agriculture and do not necessarily reflect the views of the sponsors.

Library of Congress Cataloging Card No. 94-74039
International Standard Book No. 0-309-05235-1

Additional copies of this report are available from :

National Academy Press
2101 Constitution Avenue, N.W.
Washington, D.C. 20418

©1994 by the National Academy of Sciences. All rights reserved.

No part of this book may be reproduced by any mechanical, photographic, or electronic process, or in the form of a phonographic recording, nor may it be stored in a retrieval system, transmitted, or otherwise copied for public or private use without written permission from the publisher, except for the purposes of official use by the U.S. government.

Printed in the United States of America

BOARD ON AGRICULTURE

DALE E. BAUMAN, *Chairman*, Cornell University
PHILIP H. ABELSON, American Association for the Advancement of Science, Washington, D.C.
JOHN M. ANTLE, Montana State University
WILLIAM B. DELAUDER, Delaware State University
SUSAN K. HARLANDER, Land O'Lakes, Inc., Minneapolis, Minnesota
RICHARD R. HARWOOD, Michigan State University
T. KENT KIRK, U.S. Department of Agriculture, Madison, Wisconsin
JAMES R. MOSELEY, Jim Moseley Farms, Inc., Clarks Hill, Indiana, and Purdue University
NORMAN R. SCOTT, Cornell University
GEORGE E. SEIDEL, JR., Colorado State University
CHRISTOPHER R. SOMERVILLE, Carnegie Institution of Washington, Stanford, California
PATRICIA B. SWAN, Iowa State University
JOHN R. WELSER, The Upjohn Company, Kalamazoo, Michigan

Staff

SUSAN OFFUTT, *Executive Director*
CARLA CARLSON, *Director of Communications*
JANET OVERTON, *Editor*
VIOLA HOREK, *Administrative Assistant*

The National Academy of Sciences is a private, nonprofit, self-perpetuating society of distinguished scholars engaged in scientific and engineering research, dedicated to the furtherance of science and technology and to their use for the general welfare. Upon the authority of the charter granted to it by the Congress in 1863, the Academy has a mandate that requires it to advise the federal government on scientific and technical matters. Dr. Bruce M. Alberts is president of the National Academy of Sciences.

The National Academy of Engineering was established in 1964, under the charter of the National Academy of Sciences, as a parallel organization of outstanding engineers. It is autonomous in its administration and in the selection of its members, sharing with the National Academy of Sciences the responsibility for advising the federal government. The National Academy of Engineering also sponsors engineering programs aimed at meeting national needs, encourages education and research, and recognizes the superior achievements of engineers. Dr. Robert M. White is president of the National Academy of Engineering.

The Institute of Medicine was established in 1970 by the National Academy of Sciences to secure the services of eminent members of appropriate professions in the examination of policy matters pertaining to the health of the public. The Institute acts under the responsibility given to the National Academy of Sciences by its congressional charter to be an adviser to the federal government and, upon its own initiative, to identify issues of medical care, research, and education. Dr. Kenneth I. Shine is president of the Institute of Medicine.

The National Research Council was organized by the National Academy of Sciences in 1916 to associate the broad community of science and technology with the Academy's purposes of furthering knowledge and advising the federal government. Functioning in accordance with general policies determined by the Academy, the Council has become the principal operating agency of both the National Academy of Sciences and the National Academy of Engineering in providing services to the government, the public, and the scientific and engineering communities. The Council is administered jointly by both Academies and the Institute of Medicine. Dr. Bruce M. Alberts and Dr. Robert M. White are chairman and vice-chairman, respectively, of the National Research Council.

Preface

The development of agriculture in the United States represents an unparalleled achievement in increasing the productivity of U.S. resources. Nonetheless, in the past 3 decades there has been considerable public dialogue about the unintended consequences that growth in agriculture has had for rural communities, the environment, and human health. On the threshold of a new age of farming based on innovations in biological and information technologies, rather than chemical and mechanical technologies, the agricultural research community has reason to be optimistic about the prospects for reconciling gains in agricultural productivity with a broader range of societal objectives. Success in this endeavor turns largely on the same issue as have efforts over the past century: the adequacy of scientific understanding of the fundamental processes of food and fiber production.

In 1988, the Board on Agriculture of the National Research Council decided to address, by its own initiative rather than in response to a legislative or executive branch request, a key issue for the future of agriculture—public support for agricultural research. In the process of gathering information and identifying the views of those concerned about the agricultural, food, and environmental system, the board solicited ideas from many groups, including professional scientific societies broadly related to agricultur. Following its assessment, in 1989 the board released its report *Investing in Research: A Proposal to Strengthen the Agricultural, Food, and Environmental System* (National Research Council, 1989). The report called for an increased investment in research by the U.S. Department of Agriculture (USDA) to assure attainment of three fundamental goals: (1) to maintain and increase the competitiveness of U.S. agriculture by investing in research and capitalizing on new developments in science and technology; (2) to improve human health and well-being through research advances that lead to higher quality and nutritional value in the food supply and greater food safety; and (3) to sustain the quality and productivity of natural resources—including the health of soils, the quality of the water supply and atmosphere—and preserve the biological resources that are the endowments for future generations.

The report called for an expanded federal investment in research support for agriculture, food, and the environment. It recommended an increase of $500 million to fund research through the mechanism of competitive grants administered through the USDA's Office of Science and Education. Many of the board's recommendations were initially incorporated as a presidential initiative in budget proposals and subsequently through the Food, Agriculture, Conservation, and Trade Act of 1990 (1990 farm bill) as a legislative mandate known as the National Initiative for Research on Agriculture, Food, and Environment (NRI), which along with intramural research, formula funds to the State Agricultural Experiment Stations, and grants for special research and development initiatives, provides a sound foundation for enhancing U.S. agriculture.

It has now been 5 years since the inception of the effort to build the NRI. In that time there has been significant liberalization of trade in agricultural markets important to the United States. Emphasis continues on the key role agriculture plays in assuring the health of the nation's people by providing them a safe and abundant food supply, and the need to protect the quality of the natural resources on which agriculture depends is still pressing. The contribution that high-quality science can make to fulfilling these commercial, health, and environmental goals is constrained by holding funding of the NRI at far less than the $500 million originally envisioned. The linkage between scientific opportunity and progress toward national goals was underscored by President Clinton's statement in August 1994, *Science in the National Interest* (Executive Office of the President, Office of Science and Technology Policy, 1994). Against this backdrop, the board felt it timely to contemplate the future of the NRI for the consideration of science policy makers in the Congress, the executive branch, and the public that supports and is affected by the program's results.

The board believes that it is yet too soon to conduct a comprehensive evaluation of the NRI, its program areas, and the benefits from the research it has supported. Although early results are indeed encouraging, the NRI is only now on its fourth granting cycle, and, given the lag between grant application and award decision and the start of work, only 2 years of projects have been completed. This relatively brief experience, coupled with lack of an established methodology for evaluation, meant that an assessment going beyond project description was not feasible for the board to undertake. However, it is helpful now to review the board's original recommendations made in 1989 in *Investing in Research* to assess its initial impact and to consider its implementation in the expansion of USDA competitive grants.

The board reviewed data provided by USDA's NRI program office, and it also sought, once again, the views of the agricultural and scientific community. In gathering information, the board convened a forum in October 1993 at the National Academy of Sciences' Beckman Center in Irvine, California. The board invited representatives from 69 professional scientific societies related to agriculture, food, and the environment. Participants from academia, industry, government, and nonprofit organizations were also present. It is important to note that attendees were invited to contribute and express opinions based on their personal experiences rather than on their organization's point of view.

The U.S. agricultural system has many components and serves many constituencies—consumers, agricultural and food industries, citizens concerned about the environment, agencies of the USDA and the states, other governmental departments, scientists, and colleges of agriculture and land grant universities. Often these groups express divergent priorities for agricultural research and for policy. Through a public forum, the board sought a better understanding of how the NRI has evolved in structure and function and how it might support future advances in research and address society's concerns in the broad areas of agriculture, food, and the environment.

In convening "Investing in Research: A National Research Initiative Forum," the board engaged four individuals to provide, as the basis for discussion, their views on the role of public agricultural research. The speakers were Elizabeth Anne R. Bird, Center for Rural Affairs, Walthill, Nebraska; Roger Salquist, Calgene, Inc., Davis, California; Katherine Reichelderfer Smith, Henry A. Wallace Institute for Alternative Agriculture, Greenbelt, Maryland; and William A. (Skip) Stiles, House Committee on Science, Space and Technology, U.S. Congress, Washington, D.C. The speakers' views were preceded by a historical summary of the NRI by Theodore L. Hullar, then-chair of the Board on Agriculture, and by a review of the USDA's competitive grants program and the NRI by Arthur Kelman, Chief Scientist (1991 to 1993), USDA Cooperative State Research Service National Research Initiative Competitive Grants Program.

Reflecting what was heard and discussed at the forum, the board here presents its conclusions and recommendations for the future development of the NRI. In the Executive Summary the board identifies the challenges facing the agricultural sector and highlights its recommendations. Chapter 1 provides an overview of the reasons for and context of development of the NRI program. Chapter 2 details the NRI program's content and administration. Chapter 3 offers a historical perspective of the program. Chapter 4 reemphasizes the conclusions drawn and the board's recommendations for enhancement of the

NRI program. The Appendix is a reprint of the Executive Summary from the 1989 report.

Ultimately, the board found the rationale for the establishment and vigorous expansion of the NRI more compelling than ever. Originally the board wrote (National Research Council, 1989:p. 1):

> The United States needs to invest in the future—in human capital and the scientific knowledge base—to revitalize and reinvigorate one of its leading industries, the agricultural, food, and environmental system, in its broadest sense. A sound investment strategy for research is fundamental to sustain economic performance, to respond competitively to the increased economic strengths and manufacturing capacities of other nations, and to maintain the U.S. quality of life. The commitment called for in this proposal should therefore be part of a national agenda to strengthen the United States.

The board hopes for a reinvigoration of purpose and a renewed determination to enable the NRI as an integral component of the federal scientific research portfolio to reach its objectives and enhance the agricultural system's ability to meet the needs of the next century.

Dale E. Bauman
Chairman

Contents

PREFACE v

EXECUTIVE SUMMARY 1

1 THE NATIONAL RESEARCH INITIATIVE:
  RATIONALE, DEVELOPMENT, AND CONTEXT 7

2 NRI PROGRAM CONTENT AND ADMINISTRATION 13
  Establishing a Fundamental Knowledge Base, 13
  An Expanded Program of Competitive Grants, 17
  Summary, 21

3 PROGRAM EVOLUTION 23
  Program Size, 24
  Disciplinary Emphasis, 27
  The Original Proposal, 29
  An Updated View, 30
  Sustainable Agriculture, 32

4 CONCLUSIONS AND RECOMMENDATIONS 37
  Recommendations, 38

REFERENCES 43

APPENDIX: EXECUTIVE SUMMARY FROM
INVESTING IN RESEARCH 45
    Urgency for Change, 46
    The Proposal, 48
    Rationale for the Proposal, 52
    Fiscal Realities, 56
    Conclusion, 58
    Appendix References, 59

ABOUT THE AUTHORS 61

INVESTING IN THE
NATIONAL RESEARCH
INITIATIVE

Executive Summary

In *Investing in Research: A Proposal to Strengthen the Agricultural, Food, and Environmental System* (National Research Council, 1989), the Board on Agriculture identified three major challenges facing the nation's agricultural sector. First, the competitive position of the United States, and particularly its food and fiber industries, would erode in a liberalized trading environment in the absence of market expansion and increases in productivity (i.e., gains in output achieved with fewer inputs). Second, an abundant and safe food supply of high nutritional quality would contribute significantly to the promotion of the health of the U.S. population and to the prevention of disease. Third, the imperative to protect and enhance the quality of the nation's natural resources had to be met at lowest cost to producers and consumers. The board finds these challenges no less compelling in 1994 than in 1989 and believes that success in meeting them depends in large measure on an adequate understanding of the fundamental processes of food and fiber production.

Five years ago, the board, in *Investing in Research*, recommended that

- the U.S. Department of Agriculture (USDA) investment in research should be increased to include a competitive grants program funded at $500 million annually,
- the grant program's scope should encompass six broad areas of endeavor, and
- awards should be made using four different types of grants.

The six areas of research were to include (1) plant systems; (2) animal systems; (3) nutrition, food quality, and health; (4) natural resources and the environment; (5) engineering, products, and processes; and (6) markets, trade, and policy. The four grant types were to include those to (1) individual investigators, (2) multidisciplinary teams of investigators conducting fundamental research at the intersection of disciplines, (3) multidisciplinary teams pursuing mission-linked research, and (4) institutions and individuals whose research capacity could be strengthened.

Competitive grants are not the only means by which agricultural research can or should be supported. Federal intramural agricultural research, state formula funding of agricultural research, and special grants to specific institutions for narrowly defined uses are three other parts of the USDA research program portfolio. However, the board believes competitive grants are best suited to stimulating new fundamental research activities in specific areas of science. Compared to other mechanisms, competitive grants have three major strengths that work toward attainment of the goal of stimulating advancement in fundamental areas of science, thus advancing the frontier that defines the possibilities for technological innovation.

1. Competitive grants are responsive and flexible, permitting participation of leading-edge scientists as applicants and also as proposal reviewers and allowing adjustment in year-to-year funding priorities as scientific opportunity and national need dictate.
2. Such grants can attract a broad range of scientists (from public and private, agricultural and nonagricultural institutions) to the agricultural, food, and natural-resource system, drawing talent into new endeavors and into research on unresolved problems.
3. This grant program casts a wide net that captures research proposals that will aid in developing new alliances, new initiatives, and new approaches complementary to those traditionally employed.

Contributions that are the result of competitive grants have been documented in other areas of science. Other federal agencies with strong records in meeting national needs, such as the National Institutes of Health (NIH) and the National Science Foundation (NSF), allocate more than 80 percent of research expenditures to competitive grants (National Research Council, 1994a). In contrast, competitive grants currently comprise less than 10 percent of USDA's research expenditures. The applied, regional, and site-specific nature of many food, agricultural, and environmental research and engineering issues makes it appropriate for a sizable portion of agricultural research funding to continue moving into the system through federal and state formula funds and other noncompetitive means. Clearly, there remains considerable scope for expansion of the use of competitive grants at USDA, and, equally important, of the use of peer review.

Adopted first in the president's budget proposal for fiscal year (FY) 1991, the board's recommendations in *Investing in Research* were subsequently incorporated into the Food, Agriculture, Conservation, and Trade Act of 1990 (the 1990 farm bill) as the National Initiative for Research in Agriculture, Food, and the Environment (NRI). Congressional appropriators responded to the administration's initial request for $100 million by increasing the previous year's allocation of $42.5 million to $73 million. The next year, the administration sought to add $50 million in an attempt to reach the eventual goal of a $500-million program. The NRI received $97.5 million in that year, and the amount has not increased significantly despite both the Bush and Clinton administrations' requests for funding at considerably higher levels. The design of the NRI, as recommended by the board and embodied in the farm bill, envisions a sophisticated use of innovative grants deployed across a broad spectrum of science. Consequently, the scale of the NRI's operation directly determines the scope of the research endeavor. Given that the NRI program level has hovered at about $100 million for the past 4 years, the opportunities envisioned for it have yet to be realized.

In response to the apparent stagnation in the growth of the NRI and to take stock of the experience with the NRI to date, the Board on Agriculture convened a forum in October 1993 attended by scientists and representatives from academia, industry, government, and nonprofit organizations. Although the board believed it was too soon to conduct a detailed or comprehensive evaluation of the NRI, it sought a range of opinions on the NRI's management and goals as a way of conducting informed deliberations on the possibilities for continued enhancement of the NRI. The board has taken particular note of the impediments to the NRI's growth, or the aspects of program management that might warrant strengthening, and of its support for national goals for agricultural research.

> *Given developments in international trade, medicine and health care, and environmental protection, the board finds a compelling case for increasing the current funding for the NRI to $500 million, the goal originally established.*

In restating its 1989 recommendation, the board notes that USDA research funding has grown from $1.4 billion to $1.8 billion in the intervening years. Even raising the target for competitive grants would be consistent with the board's goal of enlarging the significance of competitive grants in the overall USDA research portfolio. The original proposal would have approximately one-third of USDA research funds devoted to competitive grants, a proportion still well below that of NIH and NSF.

In *Investing in Research*, the board endorsed the need to reduce the federal budget deficit as a precondition for maintaining the health of the general economy on which the food and fiber sector depends. It suggested not only that reductions in spending on the Depression-era commodity price supports might be directed to deficit reduction but also that a portion of the savings should be invested in research. Federal outlays for these subsidies are projected to amount to $12 billion in FY 1994 and $8.5 billion in FY 1995 (Agricultural Outlook, 1994). Adherence to international trade agreements negotiated since 1989 implies the need to reduce spending further on commodity subsidies that distort markets. What better way to equip farmers to respond to market signals than to improve the efficiency of their operations? That is the fundamental reason to expand the NRI aggressively.

NRI managers have improved all aspects of the program's operation, from identification of critical research areas to composition of peer review panels. Several opportunities now exist, however, to make the NRI more accountable, effective, and relevant.

> *The board recommends that USDA research and NRI program managers pursue additional opportunities for improvement by making more systematic evaluation of program performance, redoubling efforts to promote multidisciplinary research, and continuing to assure the relevance of the NRI grant agenda to national goals.*

Although efforts must continue throughout the life of the program, particular attention should be paid now, as the NRI approaches the threshold of what the board hopes will be significant expansion.

More effort and resources should be devoted to NRI program evaluation. The board appreciates that slow growth in the NRI's funding level has resulted in stringent efforts to hold administrative costs down; however, the need for accountability argues for freeing the resourses of USDA science and education agencies to address evaluation. The NRI should initiate a vigorous effort to define key performance measures, including participation of a broadened science community. These measures should document impact on undergraduate, graduate, and postdoctoral students, and address the effectiveness of the variety of NRI grant types. Systematic documentation of scientific and broader societal benefits devised from grants supported by the NRI should be pursued. The USDA Economic Research Service should be enlisted to collaborate with NRI scientists in an effort to translate benefits into socioeconomic terms.

The NRI should pursue opportunities to promote multidisciplinary research and to expand the participation of all disciplines across program areas. Although multidisciplinary research projects are notoriously difficult to design and execute, the NRI program is addressing these difficulties and establishing a distinct multidisciplinary proposal review process. Further consideration should be given to offering planning grants to prospective research teams, to extending the funding period for multidisciplinary grants to 4 years (it is currently 3 years), and to finding innovative ways to identify individual contributions to such group efforts. At the same time, the NRI should continue its attempts to move away from equating a program area with a specific discipline. Problems in animal systems, for example, may be jointly or separately addressed by animal scientists and human nutritionists. Refinements of the requests for grant proposals and in the selection of peer reviewers will expedite integration of disciplines into work in every program area.

In carrying out the mandate to pursue research to support a sustainable food and fiber system, the board recommends that the USDA research managers continue to seek a better understanding of the relationship between individual research projects and attainment of national goals. However, the board does not believe that a single set of criteria derived from a legislative definition of sustainable agriculture will provide adequate guidance in selection of projects to support.

In 1992, USDA convened a panel to develop a sustainable agriculture "relevancy protocol" (U.S. Department of Agriculture, 1993), pursuant to farm bill guidance that, where appropriate, the NRI would support the goal of sustainability. Such a protocol would be applied to each NRI project to provide a quantitative index of its relevance to sustainable agriculture. This protocol has yet to be finalized, in large part because of controversy surrounding the definition of "sustainable agriculture" and its connections to particular research efforts. In its current version, the protocol equates relevance with a direct, near-term and positive impact on sustainable on-farm production systems. Such a restrictive view likely means a number of NRI projects would not be considered to be contributing to sustainability because it does not recognize the indirect, yet powerful contribution of much basic and applied research over the long term. Moreover, if there were exclusive focus on sustainability and emphasis of its farm bill definition on the nature of on-farm operations, research supporting better understanding of human nutrition and health, for example, would be implicitly devalued.

1

The National Research Initiative: Rationale, Development, and Context

The U.S. Department of Agriculture (USDA) was the first federal agency to sponsor extramural scientific research as mandated by the Hatch Act of 1887. However, only since 1978 has USDA employed competitive grants that rely on applicant review by scientific peers and that allow participation of those outside traditional agricultural research institutions. Until that time, USDA had funded research at its Agricultural Research Service laboratories and provided annual grants to each of 54 state agricultural experiment stations. Other public and private universities, though engaged in fundamental research important to agriculture, were generally excluded from USDA support. In response to calls for agriculture to adopt the competitive, peer-reviewed grant system used in other areas of science, authorization for such grants was introduced in the 1977 farm bill (National Research Council, 1972, 1975). However, subsequent appropriations provided only limited funding for competitive grants at USDA. The size of the grants and the range of scientific fields funded were greatly restricted in a program that received less than $50 million annually.

In 1989, the National Research Council's Board on Agriculture issued the report *Investing in Research: A Proposal to Strengthen the Agricultural, Food, and Environmental System* (National Research Council, 1989). The board recommended USDA's investment in research be increased to include a competitive grants program funded at $500 million annually, that its scientific scope be expanded into six broad areas of endeavor, and that the awards be made available through four types of grants. The six areas of research were to include plant systems; animal systems; nutrition, food quality, and health; natural resources and the environment; engineering, products, and processes; and markets, trade, and policy. The four grant types were to include those to individual principal investigators; multidisciplinary teams of investigators conducting fundamental research at the intersection of disciplines; multidisciplinary teams pursuing mission-linked research; and, institutions and individuals whose research capacity could be strengthened.

Adopted first in the president's budget proposal for fiscal year (FY) 1991, the board's recommendations were incorporated into the 1990 farm bill as the National Initiative for Research on Agriculture, Food, and the Environment (NRI). The history of funding for the NRI is chronicled in Table 1.1 as the Competitive Grants Program of USDA's Cooperative State Research Service. Congressional appropriators responded to the administration's FY 1991 request for $100 million by increasing the previous year's allocation of $42.5 million to $73 million. In FY 1992, the administration sought to add $50 million in pursuit of the goal of a $500-million competitive grants program. In spite of both Bush and Clinton administrations' requests for funding at considerably higher levels, the NRI received $97.5 million in each of FY 1992 and FY 1993 and $112.2 million in FY 1994 and a likely $103 million in FY 1995.[1]

Although growth in any federal program in an era of constrained funding is remarkable, the NRI is still far from meeting its goal of ambitious expansion. Both the Bush and the Clinton administrations specifically identified the NRI as a productive federal investment in the nation's future. The president's budget request has each year sought stronger growth in the NRI than the Congress has been willing to provide. The design of the NRI, as recommended by the board and embodied in the farm bill, envisions a sophisticated use of innovative grant mechanisms deployed across a broad spectrum of science. Consequently, the scale of the NRI's operation directly determines the scope of the research endeavor. Given that the NRI program level has not been much more than $100 million in each of the past 2 years, the opportunities envisioned for it have yet to be realized.

Though USDA's competitive grants program has doubled in size since the inception of the NRI, it accounts for less than 10 percent of the total USDA research budget of $1.8 billion annually (CRIS). Competitive grants are one of four major federal funding mechanisms for agricultural science (Table 1-1). Intramural research, conducted primarily at the facilities of the Forest Service, the Agricultural Research Service, and the Economic Research Service, receives more than one-half the USDA total, about $990 million annually

---

[1] It should be noted, however, that in some years a significant portion of these increases have not been for NRI program grants but for other competitively awarded grants, such as the U.S.-Israel Binational Agricultural Research and Development Program.

TABLE 1-1 Major USDA Funding Mechanisms for Agricultural Research

Year	Intramural				Formula		Competitive	Special		Other		Total
	ARS	FS	ERS	NAL	CSRS	ES	CSRS	CSRS	ES	CSRS	ES	
1980	358.0	95.9	35.2	7.3	152.4	200.7	15.5	15.2	78.3	2.8	6.5	967.8
1981	404.1	108.4	39.5	8.2	165.2	217.6	16.0	18.2	80.1	1.3	5.9	1,064.5
1982	423.2	112.1	39.4	8.2	180.4	232.6	16.3	23.1	76.8	0.8	6.3	1,119.2
1983	451.9	107.7	38.8	9.1	187.2	247.6	17.0	27.8	75.6	0.3	5.4	1,168.5
1984	471.1	109.4	44.3	10.4	193.6	253.2	17.0	26.5	75.6	0.6	5.5	1,207.2
1985	491.4	113.8	46.6	11.5	197.1	260.2	53.8	32.0	77.6	1.5	5.9	1,291.4
1986	483.2	113.6	44.1	10.8	189.0	260.2	48.8	30.2	78.9	1.6	5.5	1,265.9
1987	511.4	126.7	44.9	11.1	189.0	254.1	46.7	55.1	78.6	2.9	6.3	1,326.8
1988	544.1	132.5	48.3	12.2	201.8	260.8	45.4	51.8	80.2	4.1	16.9	1,398.2
1989	569.4	138.3	49.6	14.3	202.8	260.8	39.7	41.9	82.0	6.4	18.6	1,423.8
1990	593.3	150.9	51.0	14.7	202.8	265.1	42.5	73.1	86.4	8.2	18.2	1,505.7
1991	631.0	167.6	54.4	16.8	212.0	276.4	73.0	78.6	103.4	9.7	18.7	1,641.6
1992	668.4	180.5	58.7	17.8	220.3	288.5	97.5	87.1	110.0	10.6	20.9	1,760.2
1993	668.0	182.1	58.9	17.7	220.3	288.5	97.5	73.4	118.0	10.5	18.4	1,753.4
1994	691.6	192.5	55.3	18.3	225.9	298.1	112.2	72.9	117.4	12.1	19.1	1,815.3
1995[a]	708.6	204.0	53.7	19.7	225.9	298.1	130.0	29.7	121.4	1.3	13.2	1,805.6

Abbreviations: Values denote millions of dollars. ARS, Agricultural Research Service; FS, Forest Service; ERS, Economic Research Service; NAL, National Agricultural Library; CSRS, Cooperative State Research Service; ES, Extension Service.

[a] President's request.

Source: Data were provided by the USDA Office of Budget Policy Analysis.

> ### Screening for Bovine Leukemia
>
> Animals that are sick suffer unnecessarily and are less productive than those that are healthy. Treatment for disease may require medication, injected or ingested by the animal in feed. As with humans, it is the case with animals that an ounce of prevention is worth a pound of cure. Animal scientists and public health officials have consequently sought to eradicate disease (hog cholera is one success story) and to prevent its introduction to this country. However, control of many diseases still depends on understanding causes and predicting the susceptibility of animals. Bovine leukemia virus, for example, can make dairy cows severely ill or it can cause chronic infection that significantly lowers milk production. But only some cows contract leukemia. Why?
>
> NRI-supported researchers have identified the gene many cattle carry that confers resistance to this virus. The presence of this gene can be identified by testing cattle using techniques of molecular biology that examine the animals' DNA. Consequently, it should be possible to develop a screening test that allows the farmer to select for breeding those animals that will pass resistance to their offspring.

(Current Research Information System, 1994). Formula funds, for research and technology transfer and education, in the amount of about $525 million are distributed to the states each year according to formulas related to the size of farm and rural populations. Approximately one-third of the remaining $450 million is accounted for by congressional earmarks to specific research universities or entities for specific projects, and the other two-thirds to targeted federal initiatives to support international treaty obligations and the like.

So, while competitive grants are not the only mechanism for distributing allocations for agricultural research, the board argued in its earlier report that "they are best suited to stimulating new research activity in specific areas of science" (National Research Council, 1989, p. 34). The relatively small role that competitive grants plays in the USDA science funding portfolio thus results in the nation's incomplete realization of the program's unique contributions. The competitive grants mechanism was advocated in *Investing in Research* because of three major strengths that work toward attainment of the goal of stimulating advancement in new areas of science, thus pushing back the frontier on which technological innovation depends: competitive grants (1) exhibit responsiveness and flexibility, (2) attract the best talent through open competition, and (3) balance and complement research performed in other settings (through formula or special grants at universities or through intramural funds at federal facilities).

The responsiveness and flexibility of competitive grants provide the means to identify and support potentially important areas of research—areas that are emerging but that have not yet been widely recognized as significant. By drawing on leading scientists to conduct peer review of grant applications, the NRI gains a perspective on science informed by those most intimately involved with and knowledgeable about new opportunities. Responsiveness means being hospitable to—and strongly encouraging—work at the forefront of an area of science. Program announcements can be adjusted each year in response to new developments, and funding patterns thus will reflect redirection as science opportunity dictates.

Compared to other funding mechanisms, competitive grants have the potential advantage of being able to attract a broad range of scientists to the agricultural, food, and environmental system and to retain their interest. By promoting talent and openness, the NRI

- expands opportunities for scientists who are currently involved in agricultural research;
- draws productive, proven scientists from other areas, such as molecular biology or genetics, into agricultural research;
- attracts and retains younger scientists in agricultural research; and
- eases financial and institutional barriers impeding participation of women, under-represented minorities, and disabled individuals by providing them with greater opportunities for research.

Each of the four funding mechanisms now supporting agricultural, food, and environmental research has a valuable role to play in ensuring that the nation's needs are met. All four are necessary to ensure that both basic and applied research programs thrive, to support the development and transfer of new technologies, and to meet the immediate and often unpredictable needs created by agricultural pests or the vagaries of weather. Competitive grants can contribute by attracting new talent into the research system and helping agriculturalists take greater advantage of the developments rapidly occurring across all areas of science.

The contributions of competitive grants have been documented in other areas of science, such as biomedicine, that have relied extensively on competitive, peer-reviewed funding. Even at the outset of the NRI program, other federal agencies with strong records in meeting national needs allocated a much larger portion of their research and development expenditures through the competitive grants mechanism: the National Institutes of Health allocated 83 percent and the National Science Foundation, 90 percent (National Research Council, 1989, p. 37). The applied, regional, and site-specific nature of many agricultural, food, and environmental research and engineering issues makes it

> ## Combining Natural Resistance and Natural Enemies
>
> What happens when you combine a predator capable of reducing the pest population in a cotton field and a partially resistant variety of cotton that slows the pest population's growth rate? A combination of low-level resistance that synergizes and can effect a long-term decrease of possibly 60 percent in the pest population. Because pests rapidly adapt to single-gene resistance, some plant breeders now believe that partial resistance may offer long-term benefits, while single plant genes that cause high pest mortality do not. The tools of genetic engineering now offer the choice of setting levels of insect resistance high or low. Today the prime candidate genes for high or low expression are those from a bacteria that code for caterpillar- and beetle-specific toxins (i.e., Bacillus thuringiensis). The bacterial toxins have proved highly specific for targeted insect pests and are benign to humans and the environment.
>
> NRI-funded field tests have revealed synergistic interactions between natural enemies and tobacco plants (a model system) that expressed low levels of the bacterial toxin. A new computer model that simulated the synergism between the natural enemies and the partially resistant plants indicated that the presence of natural enemies may speed up, slow down, or have no effect on the rate of pest adaptation to the toxin. Ongoing research on this NRI grant is aimed at testing the results of the computer model so that problems and benefits of high and low levels of resistance can be judged more realistically. Research will focus on two of the most destructive agricultural insect pests in the United States—the Colorado potato beetle (Leptinotarsa decemlineata) and the tobacco budworm (Heliothis virescens), also known as the cotton bollworm. By developing computer models and rigorously testing predictions, scientists can offer sound advice to genetic engineers attempting to produce pest-resistant crops.

appropriate for a considerable portion of agricultural research funding to continue moving into the system through federal and state formula funds and other noncompetitive means. Nonetheless, there remains considerable scope for expanding the NRI at USDA.

2

NRI Program Content and Administration

The Board on Agriculture has argued that the NRI is a most effective way to develop the new knowledge base and human talent the agriculture industry needs to achieve national goals for health, the environment, and agriculture. Though it has yet to attain its recommended funding level, the NRI has emerged as a most dynamic component of the USDA agricultural research program. Here, the development of the program content and its administration are reviewed, starting with the USDA competitive grants program at its inception in 1978 to its expansion in and authorization as the National Research Initiative in the 1990 farm bill.

ESTABLISHING A FUNDAMENTAL KNOWLEDGE BASE

Global food shortages in the early 1970s stimulated concern about the adequacy of the scientific knowledge base as a foundation for future global food security (National Research Council, 1975, 1977). When the Congress in the 1977 farm bill directed USDA to establish a competitive grants program, its stated objective was to stimulate the development of fundamental scientific knowledge important to agriculture by adding extramural grant support—the approach used successfully by the National Science Foundation and National Institutes of Health—to the traditional USDA portfolio. However, fiscal constraints and philosophical differences within Congress and the agricultural research community on the breadth or specificity of research-program funding impeded the growth of the USDA competitive.grants program.

> ### Microbes and Soil Health
>
> Many crops are damaged by pathogenic bacteria and fungi that infect plant roots. One method of protecting crops against root pathogens involves fumigation of the soil before planting. This method is less than ideal because soil fumigants must be handled with care and do not discriminate between potentially harmful and beneficial soil organisms. Although it is known that some soils harbor soil microbes that are natural competitors of soil borne pathogens, the factors that favor the proliferation and competitiveness of these beneficial organisms are incompletely known.
>
> Research supported by the NRI has provided new information on ways to augment the organic content of soil with compost or other organic additives so as to favor the growth of beneficial microbes. At present it is still not clear what role these additives play—do they promote the growth of pathogen-killing microbes or do they directly retard the growth or attenuate the virulence of the pathogens? Understanding the factors that lead to disease suppression could allow the development of farming practices that reliably control pathogens in both specialized and diversified cropping systems.

Broad Research Program Areas or Special Grants?

Initially, the USDA competitive grants program authorized support for plant science and nutrition only. In 1985, the scope was expanded by the farm bill with a biotechnology initiative that included animal science. During its first decade, funding for competitive grants at USDA remained a minor component of USDA research expenditures, accounting for about 5 percent of the total. Within the modest dimensions of the program, philosophical differences have been reflected in the variation of focus of grant categories between quite specialized and much broader subject areas. Congressional appropriators added specific research topics in FY 1985, with new funding—$28 million—restricted for use on investigations having to do with the boll weevil/bollworm, pine bark beetle, and gypsy moth; soybean research; alcohol fuels; brucellosis; and acid precipitation. A restricted program related to problems posed by stratospheric ozone depletion, assessing the effects of ultraviolet light on crops, was added in FY 1989. Although several of these specialized and restricted programs have continued in the current NRI, a few, such as those in the three insect-specific categories, have been folded into a broader-based program on plant pest science. In general, the science community has argued that congressional appropriations should support competitive grants in broad topic ar-

TABLE 2-1 Total Federal Appropriations in Nominal Values

Year	ARS	CSRS	FS	ERS	ES	NAL	Total
1980	358.0	185.9	95.9	35.2	285.5	7.3	967.8
1981	404.1	200.7	108.4	39.5	303.6	8.2	1,064.5
1982	423.2	220.6	112.1	39.4	315.7	8.2	1,119.2
1983	451.9	232.3	107.7	38.8	328.7	9.1	1,168.5
1984	471.1	237.7	109.4	44.3	334.3	10.4	1,207.2
1985	491.4	284.4	113.8	46.6	343.7	11.5	1,291.4
1986	483.2	269.6	113.6	44.1	344.6	10.8	1,265.9
1987	511.4	293.7	126.7	44.9	339.0	11.1	1,326.8
1988	544.1	303.1	132.5	48.3	358.0	12.2	1,398.2
1989	569.4	290.8	138.3	49.6	361.4	14.3	1,423.8
1990	593.3	326.6	150.9	51.0	369.2	14.7	1,505.7
1991	631.0	373.3	167.6	54.4	398.5	16.8	1,641.6
1992	668.4	415.5	180.5	58.7	419.3	17.8	1,760.2
1993	668.0	401.7	182.1	58.9	424.9	17.7	1,753.4
1994	691.6	423.1	192.5	55.3	434.6	18.3	1,815.3
1995	708.6	386.9	204.0	53.7	432.7	19.7	1,805.6

NOTE: Values denote millions of dollars. Abbreviations: ARS, Agricultural Research Service; FS, Forest Service; ERS, Economic Research Service; NAL, National Agricultural Library; CSRS, Cooperative State Research Service; ES, Extension Service.

Source: Data were provided by the USDA Office of Budget Policy Analysis.

eas in order to generate fundamental knowledge rather than target specific problems in agriculture through the restriction of competitive grants.

The debate over the proper focus of agricultural research funding has not been strictly academic. Between FY 1980 and FY 1993, USDA outlays for agricultural research and development increased in real terms by less than 10 percent (Tables 2-1 and 2-2). Even without the claim of competitive grants on an essentially fixed budget, tension would have existed among those who advocate growth in intramural funding or increases for state formula grants or increases in special grants. Adding competitive grants to the mix during a period of revolutionary advance in biology only exacerbated the competition for support. Over the past decade, the record shows that growth in special grants and competitive grants has exceeded that in intramural support and formula grants (see Table 1-1).

TABLE 2-2 Total Federal Appropriations in Real Values

Year	ARS	CSRS	FS	ERS	ES	NAL	Total
1980	497.2	258.2	133.2	48.9	396.6	10.1	1,344.2
1981	513.5	255.0	137.7	50.2	385.8	10.4	1,352.6
1982	503.8	262.6	133.5	46.9	375.8	9.8	1,332.4
1983	515.3	264.9	122.8	44.2	374.7	10.4	1,332.3
1984	515.4	260.1	119.7	48.5	365.8	11.4	1,320.8
1985	517.3	299.4	119.8	49.1	361.8	12.1	1,359.4
1986	496.1	276.8	116.6	45.3	353.8	11.1	1,299.7
1987	511.4	293.7	126.7	44.9	339.0	11.1	1,326.8
1988	525.2	292.6	127.9	46.6	345.5	11.8	1,349.6
1989	528.2	269.8	128.3	46.0	335.2	13.3	1,320.8
1990	528.3	290.8	134.4	45.4	328.7	13.1	1,340.8
1991	543.0	321.3	144.2	46.8	342.9	14.5	1,412.7
1992	558.4	347.1	150.8	49.0	350.3	14.9	1,470.5
1993	541.8	325.8	147.7	47.8	344.6	14.4	1,422.0
1994[a]	691.6	423.1	192.5	55.3	434.6	18.3	1,815.3
1995[a]	708.6	386.9	204.0	53.7	432.7	19.7	1,805.6

NOTE: Values denote millions of dollars. Abbreviations: ARS, Agricultural Research Service; FS, Forest Service; ERS, Economic Research Service; NAL, National Agricultural Library; CSRS, Cooperative State Research Service; ES, Extension Service.

[a]Nominal values.

Source: Data were provided by the USDA Office of Budget Policy Analysis.

Program Content

The 1990 farm bill's authorization of the NRI closely followed the recommendations in the board's report (see Appendix) in terms of the six broad program areas, four grant types, and an expanded public investment to $500 million annually. In addition, the Congress specified target shares for the four grant types to include not less than 30 percent for multidisciplinary research, 20 percent for mission-linked research, and 10 percent for strengthening grants. The legislation also directed USDA to emphasize, where appropriate, research that enhanced agricultural sustainability.

AN EXPANDED PROGRAM OF COMPETITIVE GRANTS

For the first year of the NRI—FY 1991—the appropriation was $73 million. This was almost doubled from the FY 1990 appropriation for competitive grants of $42.5 million. With increased funding in FY 1991, the NRI was restructured and expanded to include four of the six recommended program divisions (plant systems; animal systems; nutrition, food quality, and health; and natural resources and the environment). Grant programs in the remaining two divisions (markets, trade, and policy; and processing for value added) were added the following year. At a program level of about $100 million over the past few years, congressional appropriations have allocated about 40 percent of the grants funded to the program area of plant systems, 25 percent to animal systems, 20 percent to natural resources, 7 percent to nutrition, and 4 percent each to processing for value added and to markets, trade, and rural development.

In implementing an expanded NRI, USDA invited the agricultural community and researchers to a series of workshops, intended to provide guidance in identifying high-priority research areas relevant for agriculture, food, and the environment. The subsequent requests for grant proposals reflected much of the advice gleaned in the workshops, including the following.

- Emphasize in instructions to reviewers—in all programs—the goal of sustainability.
- Emphasize in instructions to reviewers the goal of enhancing international competitiveness for the United States in programs such as processing for added value.
- Emphasize food safety as a critical aspect of a healthy food supply.
- Call for research on forest species in the three program areas of natural resources, plants, and processing for added value.
- Identify the need for research on global change.
- Stress the relevance of social and economic research in all the grant areas.

In recent years, the NRI has had approximately $90 million to dispense in competitive grants, after accounting for administrative expenses and funds directed for other uses. Funding is now available in each of six broad grant types. An early indicator of success of the NRI might be the interest it generates among scientists in the broad research community, whose willingness to apply for grants is a necessary, although not sufficient, condition for productive science.

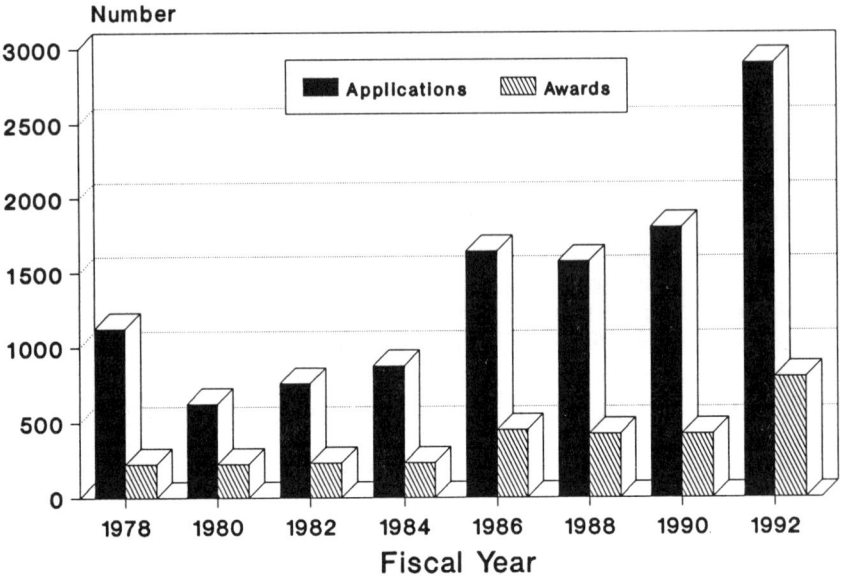

Figure 2-1 In 1978, there were 1,125 applications versus 225 awards; in 1980, 625 applications versus 225 awards; in 1982, 760 applications versus 230 awards; in 1984, 875 applications versus 230 awards; in 1986, 1,640 applications versus 450 awards; in 1988, 1,575 applications versus 425 awards; in 1990, 1,800 applications versus 425 awards, in 1992, 2,900 applications versus 800 awards. Source: Anne Datko, 1994, The National Research Iniative Competitive Grants Program, Cooperative State Research Service, U.S. Department of Agriculture, personal communication.

In each year since the inception of USDA competitive grants in the 1970s, the number of applicants has outnumbered the number of grants awarded by two-to-one and, more recently, by as much as four-to-one (Figure 2-1). After the NRI was authorized, applications increased over previous years by about one-third. Attracted by the NRI's goal of increasing the size of each grant made (as well as the overall number), scientists have requested, in aggregate, more than five times the amount actually available for grants (Figure 2-2).

This high demand for NRI grants has persisted in recent years despite the imposition by congressional appropriators of a cap on the allowable indirect cost that can be included in each grant. Capping the reimbursement to the home university may increase the amount available to the investigator, but the costs must be absorbed by the institution nonetheless. So, the cap on indirect costs may either be viewed as a way of leveraging limited NRI funds or as a way to achieve cost-sharing with participating universities. If this latter per-

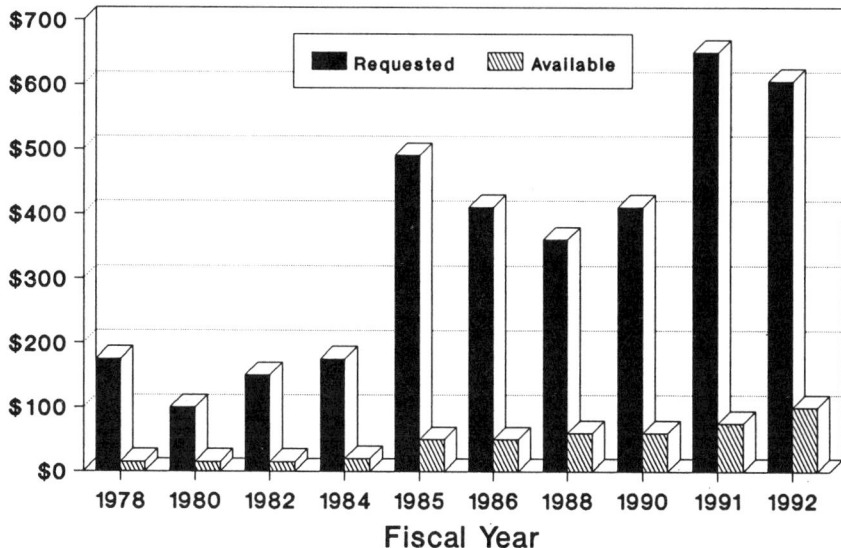

Figure 2-2 In 1978, requested amounts (in millions of dollars) totaled $175 versus $15 available funds; in 1980, $100 requested versus $15 available; in 1982, $150 requested versus $15 available; in 1984, $175 requested versus $20 available; in 1985, $490 requested versus $50 available; in 1986, $360 requested versus $60 available; in 1990, $410 requested versus $60 available; in 1991, $650 requested versus $75 available, in 1992, $605 requested versus $100 available. Source: Anne Datko, 1994, The National Research Iniative Competitive Grants Program, Cooperative State Research Service, U.S. Department of Agriculture, personal communication.

spective is true, then it might be that the number of NRI applicants would be even higher if it were not for the cap on indirect costs. Anecdotal evidence supports the perception that it is investigators at private universities who are most likely to have decided against applying for the restrictive NRI grants.

The identities of those who do not apply for NRI grants are, of course, difficult to discern, but the institutional affiliations of those who do apply is as follows: slightly less than 75 percent come from land grant colleges and universities; private and other public institutions submit about 16 percent of all applications; federal laboratories (mostly those of the Agricultural Research Service and the Forest Service) submit about 6 percent of the total; the remaining 5 percent of individuals come from industry and other nongovernmental research organizations (Figure 2-3). In general, grants are awarded to each

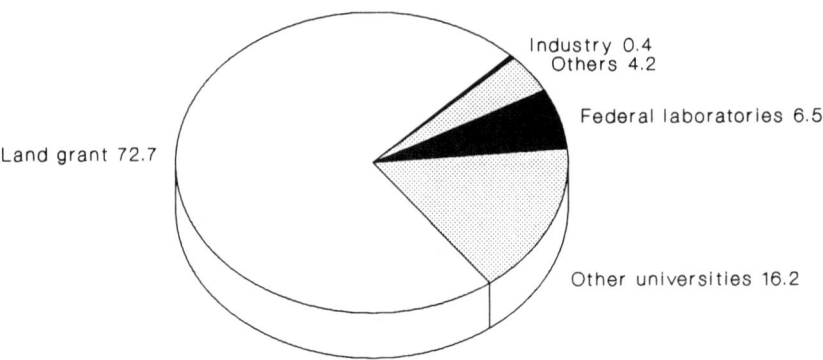

Figure 2-3 Institutional affiliations of those applying for NRI grants for fiscal year 1993. Values are percentages. Source: Source: Anne Datko, 1994, The National Research Iniative Competitive Grants Program, Cooperative State Research Service, U.S. Department of Agriculture, personal communication.

type of organization in about the same proportion as represented by applications.

In the pool of applicants each year, about two-thirds are submitting new proposals (Figure 2-4). Another one-fifth are turning in proposals revised in response to peer reviews of an earlier submission. About one-tenth are seeking renewal of multiyear projects. In FY 1993, some 30 panels of peer scientists were assembled to review about 3,000 grant applications. Ultimately, just under 800 grants were funded at an average of $110,000 each.

The contribution of the NRI's extensive review process to the quality of science should not be overlooked. Although aimed directly at the proposals submitted, a reviewer's constructive criticism improves an investigator's understanding of the chosen research field as well as the methodology of investigation. Likewise, participation as a peer reviewer maintains a scientist's incentive to remain abreast of developments in a scientific field. And, as noted in *Investing in Research*, the system of peer review promotes communication and links across scientific disciplines and between program sectors. Individuals from all segments of the scientific community—academia, industry, and government—come together to discuss and refine program priorities, establish proposal review criteria, and serve on peer review panels.

In FY 1993, $92 million was awarded in 790 grants in six program areas. Two-thirds of the total funding supported fundamental research and the other

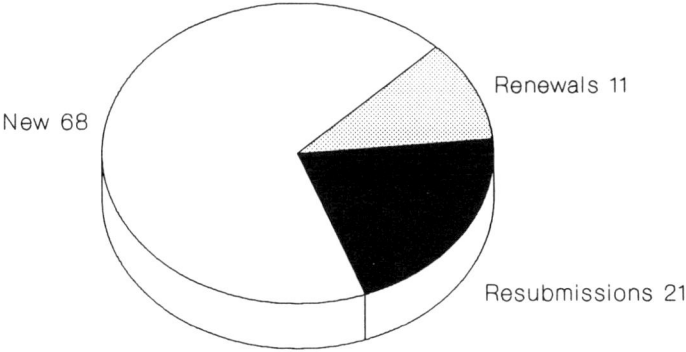

Figure 2-4 Number of new, resubmitted, and renewed applications for NRI grants for fiscal year 1993. Values are percentages. Source: Source: Anne Datko, 1994, The National Research Iniative Competitive Grants Program, Cooperative State Research Service, U.S. Department of Agriculture, personal communication.

one-third supported mission-linked research. Similarly, two-thirds of the funds went to single-discipline grants and another one-third to multidisciplinary grants. It is not the case, however, that all the fundamental science grants were awarded to single-discipline projects or that all the mission-linked proposals were multidisciplinary. The NRI design provides for fundamental and applied research by multidisciplinary teams.

SUMMARY

Both the traditional agricultural and the broader scientific research communities have demonstrated interest in competing for grants under the NRI. Although it is a straightforward matter to document the volume of grant applications, judgments about quality are necessarily more subjective. There is consensus among NRI staff and panel members and managers that "good to high" characterizes the overall quality and relevance of the proposals being received and that the quality has been increasing each year. The failure of a scientist to receive funding is not necessarily an indication that a poor proposal was submitted. The judgment is that, in most program areas, increased funding would at least double the acceptance rate. To date, scientists at the land rant institutions have been the major beneficiaries of the NRI, but as awareness of the program's existence spreads, broader participation can be expected, especially with continued growth in the funds available in total and with a resolution of the restriction on indirect cost reimbursement.

3

Program Evolution

In comparison with other federal agricultural programs, the NRI is both very young and very small. Inevitably, experience will dictate the need for modifications in both administration and program content. The NRI chief scientists and staff members have engaged those within and outside the research community who express concerns about the development of the NRI. At times, it may appear that the attention the NRI receives is out of proportion to its size in the USDA research budget ($100 million out of $1.8 billion annually). However, focus on the NRI—sometimes, it seems, to the exclusion of intramural, formula, and special grants—is emblematic of the recognition that competitive grants are a powerful tool supporting development of science and technologies that will carry agriculture into the next century. The NRI is indeed a high-stakes investment.

Still, the board finds there are some critical concerns that transcend the category of "growing pains" for the NRI. In the forum it held in October 1993, the board made a particular effort to explore these ideas, which may be characterized as follows:

- Does the small size of the NRI indicate that it has minor impact on progress in agricultural science? Is there a means for evaluating systematically the contributions made by the NRI to demonstrate its current role and future potential?
- Do the current program areas encourage inordinate reliance on single-discipline approaches to research that impede innovation and reduce

relevance? In particular, is there a broader role for the social sciences?
- If a specific-discipline approach is overemphasized, are the provisions for multidisciplinary research correspondingly under emphasized? How might such an imbalance be rectified?
- In order to carry out the congressional mandate, should the evaluation of each grant application explicitly include its contribution to sustainability as a paramount criterion for determining acceptance? How should the mandate be addressed?

PROGRAM SIZE

The NRI is, as has been noted above, a small part of all USDA research expenditures and an even smaller part of all U.S. spending for agricultural research, including federal and state programs and those of the private sector. At its current scale, can the program be said to contribute in a major way to the advancement of scientific knowledge about agriculture? At the forum, Roger Salquist, the chief executive officer of Calgene, observed, "Quite simply, it's too little money and too diffuse." Compared to the scale of other public and private research investments, the parceling out of an average of 800 grants of $125,000 for a duration of about 2 years or less seems modest. Although private agricultural and biotechnology firms understand the importance of publicly funded research, the NRI may not figure as prominently as established programs, such as formula funds, if at all, in their perception of the public system's contribution to scientific innovation.

Evaluating the Significance of NRI

The answer to the question about the significance of the NRI is straightforward. Investments in agricultural research have been shown to yield returns in excess of 40 percent (Alston et al., 1994), with the stream of returns occurring some years after the initial research investment has been made and new technologies have been developed and adopted. Consequently, the benefits of the recent NRI grants will be realized in future years, and, using the past as a guide, these gains will be large. However, as with any investment, larger principal yields larger returns, and the overall size of the NRI constrains the magnitude of its contribution to national goals for agriculture, human health, and the environment.

Although rate-of-return analyses demonstrate impressive returns to agricultural research measured in the aggregate, there are other ways that the contributions of the NRI could be evaluated. To date, few of the administrative resources available to the NRI have been devoted to tracking its output, although its output could be easily documented. For example, success in stimu-

> ### Antimicrobial Activity in Food Processing
>
> Whether in a home kitchen or an industrial-scale processing plant, potentially harmful microorganisms can find their way to the surfaces and utensils used in preparing food. Instructions to the consumer about handling raw poultry, for example, reflect concern that the microbial contaminants killed when the meat is cooked might remain on knives, countertops, or cutting boards used to prepare the raw bird. Other foods might pick up these microbes if surfaces have not been adequately cleaned. Although the time-honored approach to sanitation prescribes use of soap and disinfectant chemicals, an alternative might lie in the natural ability of some bacteria to destroy harmful microbes.
>
> Supported by NRI grants, scientists are studying new uses for the antimicrobial proteins produced by bacteria used to make cheese from milk. One of these proteins, called nisin, shows promise when applied to cooking surfaces; its antimicrobial activity appears to be stable and may even last after the surface has been washed. Although questions remain about how to use such bacteria on a large scale, understanding the fundamental processes by which the bacteria attack microbes will provide invaluable guidance in practical applications.

lating and supporting new and better science could be shown by keeping track of the number of peer-reviewed publications that resulted from NRI-funded research. Another measure of the impact of the NRI on the overall productivity of the science community might be the number of postdoctoral researchers who receive support from an NRI grant as well as the number of undergraduate and graduate students who are able to become involved in research as a result of NRI funding. The availability of NRI funds may help scientists leverage support from home institutions or other funding agencies, and it might be possible to measure this success by noting each grant proposal's identification of other sources of funds. In terms of contributions to technological development, the number of technology licenses and patents granted based on NRI research would provide evidence of its value.

In 1989, the board identified a series of questions that could be central to ongoing evaluations. Judgments about the ultimate quality of the scientific contribution can only be made as time goes by, as discussed. However, intermediate progress could be examined.

- Are science and technology priorities within the major program areas defined insightfully and do they relate to national needs?

> ## Genetic Disease Resistance
>
> Plants are susceptible to destructive infections from a wide variety of viral, bacterial, fungal, and nematode species. For many modern cultivars, breeders incorporate genetic resistance to pathogen. In many cases, however, pathogens rapidly develop new virulence traits that permit them to overcome the effects of disease resistant genes. Because the mechanism of genetic disease resistance was not known, it was not possible to explore the development of stable genetic disease resistance.
>
> During the past year, NRI-sponsored research has led to a major breakthrough in understanding the molecular basis of genetic disease resistance. Genes that condition resistance to viral, fungal, and bacterial diseases in four species of plants have been cloned by several different laboratories pursuing different approaches to the problem. An exciting finding was the observation that all of the genes encode proteins with common structural features. This raises the possibility that many forms of disease resistance have a common underlying mechanism. It may be that these genes can be used to isolate the corresponding resistance genes from most or all species of higher plants. They also may be directly useful in creating a new spectrum of disease resistance by genetic engineering. More important, the availability of the genes permits the use of powerful new experimental approaches to understanding the mechanisms involved in disease resistance.

- Are researchers from across the entire science and technology community seeking grants and submitting high-quality proposals?
- Is the program effectively linked to, and does it routinely communicate with, other USDA programs, those of other federal science agencies, state programs, and the private sector?

There are, no doubt, other ways to assess the NRI's contribution, including the descriptions of individual research projects and their connections to better science and to improved performance and sustainability of the agricultural system. The board believes that if USDA were to request funds for—or reallocation of resources to—documenting achievements of the NRI, it would be a worthwhile investment that could help bolster support for its growth by demonstrating the benefits it provides.

Garnering Funds

In a time of federal fiscal restraint, additional funding for the NRI will come only from redirection of spending on other activities. The board has made clear its view that expansion of the NRI competitive-grants program should not come at the expense of other agricultural research carried out intramurally or in universities. As a category, agricultural research consistently provides large returns to farmers and to consumers; it would be unwise to reduce funding of such a productive investment. However, there may be other areas of federal spending for which the returns to the nation are lower or for which the original purpose has been served. In *Investing in Research*, the board suggested that the outlays currently devoted to the commodity price support programs might be targeted for reduction, with part of the savings going to reduce the federal deficit and part going to reinvestment in a high-return program—the NRI. U.S. agriculture is entering an era of liberalized world trade in commodities and agricultural products; decades-old price-support programs may be dismantled to comply with new trading rules. But the need to maintain the competitiveness of the agricultural sector is as compelling as ever. Only now, with increased reliance on the marketplace rather than on government subsidies, that competitive edge is maintained by gains in productivity, in holding down the costs of production while protecting environmental quality. Ultimately, productivity gains depend on advances in science and translation into new technologies. From this perspective, the NRI will be a part of the foundation for future U.S. success in international markets.

DISCIPLINARY EMPHASIS

The NRI funds research in six broad categories: (1) natural resources and environment; (2) nutrition, food quality, and health; (3) animal systems; (4) plant systems; (5) markets, trade, and (5) policy; and processing for value-added products. Some critical observers have described the program as divided into areas that represent a particular discipline or group of disciplines. For example, animal systems research is addressed by animal scientists; nutrition, food quality, and health are addressed by nutritionists and food scientists; and natural resources and the environment by soil scientists and ecologists. Critics charge that although the NRI program has been set up to avoid sorting research proposals into disciplinary compartments, efforts have not been entirely successful. They point out that only the program area for markets, trade, and policy has been perceived as the realm of social scientists.

According to NRI program data, it is indeed the case that the markets, trade, and policy grants division has been dominated by social scientists in writing requests for proposals, submitting proposals, and participating on peer review panels. For the purposes of this discussion, the social sciences are defined as those that study human systems, human institutions, and human behaviors. These disciplines include economics, human ecology, sociology, psychology, anthropology, political science, and rural and community development.

Those who argue for an expanded role for the social sciences do not necessarily advocate increased funding within the markets, trade, and policy division but rather for greater participation across all six NRI program areas. Kitty R. Smith, director of Policy Studies at the Wallace Institute for Alternative Agriculture, summarized this view in her remarks at the board's October 1993 forum.

> Segregating the social sciences has the effect of discouraging, or at least not actively encouraging, research proposals that address the human behavioral or institutional aspects of social problems relating to the natural or physical science systems. This is a problem because the direct and immediate, or eventual and potential contributions of NRI-funded research to the resolution of social concerns is the very basis of public research support, and one that we need to preserve in order to see a growth in that funding. It is humans who value environmental quality; it is humans who manage plant and animal systems for agricultural purposes; it is humans who are increasingly concerned about food quality and safety. It is also these same humans who act as constituents of the public policy officials who are making agricultural research funding decisions.

It is also the case that social science research can help identify and quantify the benefits that the NRI brings to consumers, to farmers, and to industry.

The association of issue areas with particular disciplines exists despite efforts of the NRI program to design requests for proposals to avoid it and is certainly not unique to the NRI. The concentration of the social scientists' participation in one grant category indicates a lack of complete success in this regard. Critics argue that the association of NRI program areas with particular disciplines constrains the contributions of more than just the social sciences. In this view, the assumption of a disciplinary focus by issue area leads to competition among disciplines and to factionalism that inhibits the advance of science and, not coincidentally, of the NRI itself. Further, it may well be that disciplinary compartmentalization, whether real or perceived, precludes innovation that stems from the attempt to address problems that cross disciplinary boundaries.

Multidisciplinary Research

In its 1989 proposal for an expanded competitive grants program, the board argued that an enhanced program would provide significant new opportunities for supporting multidisciplinary research. Such work combines expertise from two or more disciplines into a shared focus on a common research

> ### Ecology, Community, and Infrastructure in the Imperial Valley
>
> History has shown that civilizations dependent on irrigated agriculture have collapsed, although precisely why remains largely a mystery. An opportunity for "real time" archeology exists today: California's Imperial Valley is the single largest and oldest example of irrigated agriculture in the United States. Along with other irrigated areas of the West, the region has experienced ecological crises, declines in economic activity and the viability of communities, and changes in the availability of irrigation water and in other circumstances of commodity production.
>
> Research supported by the NRI will consider, from a sociological perspective, how the Valley's ecology, human communities, and physical infrastructure have developed. Analysis will focus on understanding stresses attributable to the increasing costs of maintaining agriculture and the natural environment and of acquiring farm labor and protecting human health. Better understanding of these complex interrelationships could assist in devising public and private strategies for managing the fragile natural resources on which a historically productive agriculture has been based.

problem that has an integrated plan of study. A multidisciplinary project requires research *in* the disciplines and at the same time draws research and results *from* the disciplines to form a study that integrates both the disciplines and the results to examine systematically the various facets as well as the totality of the problem. As used here, *multidisciplinary* research designates both *cross-disciplinary* and *interdisciplinary* research, even though the three terms have somewhat different meanings (National Research Council, 1989). For example, developing sustainable animal agricultural systems requires research in agronomy and soil science, ecology and ecosystems analysis, engineering, animal nutrition, population and community biology, and economics, at a minimum.

THE ORIGINAL PROPOSAL

Investing in Research recommended that to realize the full potential of science and technology in agricultural, food, and environmental research, the USDA competitive grants program should direct up to 50 percent of its support to multidisciplinary research, through multidisciplinary team grants, both fundamental and mission-linked. This emphasis is meant to stimulate more multidisciplinary team research and to encourage it strongly among senior scientists. The report describes two types of multidisciplinary research: (1) fundamental multidisciplinary team grants, conceived of as the involvement of at least two senior scientists as principal investigators; and (2) multidisciplinary, mission-linked teams involving about four senior scientists.

The board recognized that encouraging and evaluating multidisciplinary research would not be easy. In particular, it noted that multidisciplinary team research presents a number of conceptual and practical difficulties. Chief among them are issues of leadership, management, coordination, rewards, and satisfaction. In addition, granting agencies have customarily awarded grants to single investigators within one scientific discipline; thus, the reviewing mechanisms are generally organized on a single-discipline basis. Involving reviewers from several different disciplines is considerably more difficult. "Notwithstanding the difficulties, multidisciplinary research is clearly worth doing because of the multifaceted nature of the problems—both the fundamental and the more applied problems that are common in the agricultural, food, and environmental system. It is also worthwhile because of the unexpected synergism and creativity that good collaboration may generate," the board concluded (National Research Council, 1989, p. 40).

AN UPDATED VIEW

The board originally recommended that 50 percent of all grants be multidisciplinary awards. In FY 1993, multidisciplinary awards represented 34 percent of total NRI grants. Clearly, constraints on total funding jeopardize growth in this activity, but it is just as important to ensure that the grants supported do indeed represent productive investments. It is noteworthy that in 1993, NRI, in cooperation with the National Science Foundation and the Department of Energy, initiated a joint program on collaborative research. This is a positive step, but a number of issues concerning multidisciplinary research will require ongoing assessment. Although these are discussed in context to the NRI, such impediments may be characteristic of multidisciplinary work under any circumstances.

The Review Process

Broad, multidisciplinary projects are intrinsically difficult to review. Frequently, two or three study groups must evaluate a project, thus requiring that it pass muster more than once. With existing funding constraints, this situation of "double jeopardy" unfairly decreases the probabilities of approval, while increasing the administrative costs of review. To the extent that industry faces the need to conduct and expeditiously evaluate the prospects for multidisciplinary research, the advice of experienced private firms might be sought by NRI managers as an additional source of expertise.

Start-Up Logistics

Time and energy are required to assemble multidisciplinary teams. Each expert on the team must become familiar with the language and culture of the others, and frequently, adjustments must be made to smooth over any differences. The start-up of a multidisciplinary team presents two difficulties: (1) bringing the team together to write a fundable proposal and (2) finding ways to keep the team working together efficiently. One option that might further encourage multidisciplinary proposals is to formulate a modest planning grant with a 1-year duration. Planning grants would be aimed primarily at proposal assembly but in some cases might include preliminary experiments or data collection.

Funding

Typically, multidisciplinary studies require more funding per year than single-discipline studies, and funding needs are increased by their typically longer duration. Reviewers, study groups, and grant managers sometimes are reluctant to recommend funding of a large study when that level of funding could instead support two or three smaller studies. Underfunding of multidisciplinary projects is counterproductive. Funding is usually needed for 4 to 5 years because of the investment of time at start-up as well as time at the end of the study to integrate data.

Incentives and Rewards

Contributions of some team members, especially beginning or untenured scientists, can become buried in large, multidisciplinary projects, particularly if one or two of the other participants are established senior investigators. Mechanisms are needed to identify roles clearly, especially in publications. Department heads, division leaders, and tenure committees need to be sensitive to issues involving individual contributions to multidisciplinary projects and appropriately supportive of the scientists pursuing multidisciplinary studies. Mechanisms for continuing funding for multidisciplinary studies are not yet optimal. Continuation grants for single-discipline studies are common if excellent work is being done. Continuation grants for multidisciplinary studies can be more difficult to achieve because of the inherent delays encountered when multiple groups must collate and evaluate data, prepare and approve publications, and work through other project-related issues jointly. Criteria for evaluating multidisciplinary projects might be somewhat modified compared with standard evaluations. For example, meeting milestones might substitute in part for timely publications. Failure to have continued funding would be detrimental to young scientists just beginning their careers.

Training in Multidisciplinary Research

Multidisciplinary research can provide unusually good opportunities for graduate and postdoctoral training. However, successful multidisciplinary projects usually will consist of personnel with reasonable depth of expertise in their particular areas. In other words, breadth of interest cannot substitute for the competence a scientist needs to contribute his or her component of a project. Therefore, students need to be trained to be competent in the primary discipline first and co-disciplines second.

SUSTAINABLE AGRICULTURE

As debate about the provisions of the 1990 farm bill progressed, it became clear that interest in the research title transcended the usual constituency of federal and university researchers. Groups with broad interests in promoting the well-being of farmers, rural communities, and the environment came to see the significance of science and technology in furthering their goals. The bill's language ultimately reflected their influence in the definition of sustainable agriculture (PL 95-113, 91 Stat. 981, 7USC 3101, Sec. 1404(17)):

> . . . an integrated system of plant and animal production practices having a site-specific application that will, over the longer-term
>
> A) satisfy human food and fiber needs;
> B) enhance environmental quality and the natural resource base upon which the agricultural economy depends;
> C) make the most efficient use of nonrenewable resources and on-farm resources and integrated, where appropriate, natural biological cycles and controls;
> D) sustain the economic viability of farm operations; and
> E) enhance the quality of life for farmers and society as a whole . . .

More specific to the NRI, the 1990 farm bill also directed the Secretary of Agriculture to ensure that competitive grants awarded are, where appropriate, consistent with the development of systems of sustainable agriculture.

Since the passage of the 1990 farm bill, the NRI managers have carried on a dialogue with those who spearheaded the successful effort to introduce the goal of sustainability explicitly. Active in this dialogue has been the Sustainable Agriculture Coalition, whose membership includes the Center for Rural Affairs (CRA), among others. Speaking at the October 1993 forum, Elizabeth Bird of the CRA summarized the Sustainable Agriculture Coalition's consensus view and identified two ways for research to support the development of sustainable agricultural systems: (1) focus on sustainable agricultural systems that use an interdisciplinary approach and (2) target component or reductionist research toward the concerns of those practicing or researching sustainable agricultural systems. She further explained,

> Since the NRI's inception in the 1990 farm bill, we have been advocating for a full implementation of the congressional mandate for mission-linked systems research and for multidisciplinary research. The publication of the 1994 "Request for Proposals" represents a major step forward in the realization of our vision for the NRI. But for us, this is not yet the end of the story. In addition to our support for fuller attention to mission-linked and multidisciplinary research, we have advocated strongly for the NRI to emphasize basic research that will simultaneously be useful to environmental sustainability and to moderate-scale farming opportunities.

In its publication *Sustainable Agriculture in the National Research Initiative* (Center for Rural Affairs, 1991), the CRA outlined its suggestions for ways to ensure that the NRI program emphasizes sustainable agriculture. Requests for grant proposals should seek research that relates to the goals of sustainable agriculture. As the CRA interprets these goals, NRI research should, among other things,

- expand economic opportunities in the rural United States including self-employment opportunities in family farming and rural communities;
- strengthen the family-farm system, primarily "small"- and "moderate"-sized, owner-operated farms;
- enhance the farmer's use of his or her labor and management skills; and
- facilitate the use of resources that can be generated directly on the farm or in the local community rather than somewhere else in the state, nation, or world.

The CRA argues that in implementing these goals, proposal review should explicitly address relevance to sustainability. The coalition further asserts that such relevance, and not scientific merit, should be the paramount consideration in awarding grants.

A Relevancy Protocol

Implementation of the congressional mandate to support sustainable agriculture falls to USDA's research agencies. In July 1992, the Cooperative State Research Service and the Agricultural Research Service jointly convened a panel to develop a sustainable agriculture relevancy protocol. In 1993 USDA issued "Relevancy of AES [Agricultural Experiment Station] Research to Sustainable Agriculture" (U.S. Department of Agriculture, 1993). The protocol would be applied to each project funded by the NRI to provide a measure, using a quantitative index, of its relevancy to sustainable agriculture. This protocol has yet to be finalized and has never been used by USDA in the evaluation of NRI grant applications, in large part because of the controversy surrounding the definition of "sustainable agriculture" and its connection to particular research efforts.

For those responsible for carrying out the charge, the design and use of a relevancy protocol creates concerns. Such a protocol assumes—without corroborative testing, evaluation, or necessary agreement on defining relevance to sustainable agriculture—that projects can be assessed and quantified as being consistent or inconsistent with sustainable agriculture. Panels composed of individuals representing different perspectives on sustainability are assembled to apply the protocol to individual projects, with the final rating calculated as an average of the panel members' subjective opinions. Lacking an objective basis for relating this rating to well-defined outcomes, it will not be possible to assess whether the protocol will help select projects that are consistent with the development of systems of sustainable agriculture.

Another concern is related to the appropriate use of sustainability protocol in evaluating NRI projects. The goals of the NRI are consistent with the broad purpose of establishing a sustainable food and fiber system. However, when the protocol requires that a research project have *direct* impact on a sustainable system, much potential for the gains resulting from research go unrecognized. Under the proposed protocol scoring system, a project without direct (presumably near-term) impact is judged as neutral with respect to the goal of sustainability. NRI managers believe many competitive grant proposals would fall into the "no direct impact" category, which has been assigned a numerical score of zero by the protocol. (Positive scores are assigned to projects judged to have direct impact; negative scores to those judged detrimental.) Even though projects may have the *potential* to support sustainability, the implication of the current scoring system is that they do not contribute.

The farm bill directs use of the sustainability criteria where relevant, and the board believes that the definition of relevance has not yet been settled in a way that permits straightforward use of a protocol. Recognition of the longer-term, indirect, and often powerful influence of much basic and applied science mitigates against the possibility that a conclusive, all-purpose protocol can be devised. If there were exclusive focus on sustainability of family farms and primary emphasis of its farm bill definition on the nature of on-farm operations, much research supporting better understanding of human nutrition and health, for example, would be implicitly devalued. Although the aim of the NRI should be to avoid engagement in projects that detract from the possibilities for sustainability, there are other worthy goals recognized by the Congress that enhance the well-being of the nation's people and natural resources. Skip

Program Evolution

Stiles, of the House Committee on Science, Space, and Technology, told the October 1993 forum audience of the need to link research efforts "more closely to national needs in order to regain strong public support." So, while exclusive focus on sustainability might be inappropriate, serious consideration of the NRI's contribution to broad public policy goals would, by Stiles' reasoning, certainly be in order.

4

Conclusions and Recommendations

In 1989, the Board on Agriculture identified three major challenges facing the nation's agricultural sector (National Research Council, 1989). In 1994, the board finds these challenges no less compelling.

First, the competitive position of the United States, and particularly its food and fiber industries, would erode in a liberalized trading environment unless productivity increased and market opportunities expanded. Competitiveness in international markets has continued to be of paramount concern to the U.S. farm and food sector. Domestic demand for food rises only slowly with population growth; yet the productive capability of U.S. agriculture and industry continues to increase, enabling it to provide food and fiber to other nations at low cost. In this hemisphere, international trade rules were rewritten to promote open markets under the North American Free Trade Agreement. Ratification of the results of the Uruguay Round of the General Agreement on Tariffs and Trade will extend similar liberalization around the globe. In the future, the ability of U.S. agriculture to capitalize on trade opportunities will depend less on subsidization by the federal government than on continued gains in the sector's productivity.

The importance of scientific advance to the nation's well-being was recently affirmed by The White House in the first major post-Cold War review of national policy. In the report "Science in the National Interest" (Executive Office of the President, Office of Science and Technology Policy, 1994)," the Clinton administration asserted,

> Scientific knowledge is necessary for helping us achieve our national goals of improved health, environment, prosperity, national security, and quality of life. ... Success in this effort demands sustained commitment to fundamental science, the foundation on which technical progress ultimately rests.

In agriculture, for example, technical progress in pest control, based on gains in the understanding of mechanisms of disease resistance, can enhance a farmer's ability to manage risk. Such advances can enable farmers to meet growing world food needs and also lay the foundation for transfer of knowledge to other countries to develop their own economies.

Second, an abundant and safe food supply of high nutritional quality contributes significantly to the promotion of the health of the U.S. population and to the prevention of disease. The well-being of U.S. citizens is greatly affected by their nutritional status. A good diet promotes health and helps prevent disease. U.S. citizens need foods that are affordable and convenient to prepare and consume, yet safe and of high nutritional quality. Improvements in basic crop and livestock products as well as processed foods can contribute to improvements in the diets of the entire U.S. population.

Third, the imperative to protect and enhance the quality of the nation's natural resources on which agriculture depends must be addressed at lowest cost to producers and consumers. Unless the quality of its soil and water are protected, the United States cannot hope to sustain its agricultural productivity, let alone its standard of living, into the future. Certain farming, ranching, and forestry practices can degrade the environment, and it is of utmost importance that alternative management systems based on sound research be developed. The Board on Agriculture recently released two reports that consider how these goals might be attained, *Soil and Water Quality: An Agenda for Agriculture* (National Research Council, 1993) and *Rangeland Health* (National Research Council, 1994b).

RECOMMENDATIONS

To meet the challenges of (1) competitiveness, (2) providing an abundant and high-quality food supply, and (3) improving the state of our natural resources, the board proposed a reinvigoration of the nation's agricultural research program to be accomplished through a significant expansion of the role of competitive grants in the traditional USDA funding portfolio. The rationale and strategy for the effort were described in *Investing in Research* (National Research Council, 1989), which provided a blueprint that was subsequently adopted by the USDA and codified by the Congress in the 1990 farm bill as the NRI.

Today, the board finds that the NRI has yet to reach the potential envisioned for it. This reflects the fact that the original recommendation—to devote $500 million annually to competitive grants—has not been reached; indeed, the funding level has hovered at about $100 million for 3 years. Without aggressive expansion, a significant portion of the benefit of new science and technology will go unrealized, and the nation's goals for enhanced competitiveness, improved health, and environmental quality will be more difficult to attain.

The board's original recommendation for the expanded use of competitive research grants in agricultural science recognized how productive that mechanism had proved in medicine and other areas of science. More extensive use of competitive grants would complement the science done elsewhere in the traditional agricultural research system, at federal facilities, and at land grant universities and colleges. Furthermore, it was the board's hope that the opportunities for all agricultural science would be increased by extending the offer of participation to the broader scientific community. The opportunities for such significant return on an investment of taxpayer money continue to exist today.

Funding

The board reemphasizes—given the developments in international trade, health care, and environmental protection—the critical importance of achieving the original funding goal of $500 million. It again reiterates, however, that the increment in NRI funding should not come at the expense of other federal agricultural research support.

In restating its 1989 recommendation of a $500 million level for the NRI, the board notes that, in total, USDA research funding has grown from $1.4 billion to almost $1.8 billion in the intervening years. Even raising the target for competitive grants beyond $500 million would be consistent with the board's goal of enlarging the significance of competitive grants in the overall USDA research portfolio. The original proposal implied that about one-third of total USDA research funds would be devoted to competitive grants, a proportion still well below that of the National Institutes of Health and the National Science Foundation.

In *Investing in Research*, the board argued that significant expansion in competitive grants funding (from $42.5 million to $500 million) could be justified on at least two counts. First was the high rate of return to investment in agricultural research, estimated to range between 45 and 130 percent. These returns translate into benefits for natural resource management, nutritional status of the people of the United States, and the nation's competitiveness in international markets. Second, the board said that "current funding for the agricultural research system cannot adequately support either the in-depth studies or the broad scope of science and technology necessary to maintain the competitiveness and sustainability of the overall agricultural, food and environmental system." The $500-million target was selected, at least in part, because the board felt confident the pool of talented scientists was large enough to put such an expanded program to good use—a judgment proved sound by the subsequent surge of quality competitive grant applications. Although raising the target to $750 million, for example, would reinforce for the entire research community the importance of fundamental, peer-reviewed agricultural science, the board recognizes the more immediate need to reach the original goal of $500 million. As the overall agricultural research funding level has grown, $500 million in competitive grants would, at a minimum, maintain some degree of balance in the USDA portfolio.

In *Investing in Research*, the board endorsed the need to reduce the federal budget deficit as a precondition for maintaining the health of the general economy on which the food and fiber sector depends. It suggested that reductions in spending on the Depression-era commodity price supports might be directed to deficit reduction but that a portion of the savings might go to investment in research. Federal outlays for these subsidies amounted to $12 billion in FY 94 and $8.5 billion in FY 95 (Agricultural Outlook, 1994). Adherence to international trade agreements negotiated since 1989 implies the need to reduce spending further on commodity subsidies that distort markets. Clearly the better way to equip producers to respond to market signals rather than to government edicts is to improve the efficiency of their operations. That is the fundamental reason to expand aggressively the NRI.

Evaluation, Multidisciplinary Research, and Relevancy

Any investment of public resources requires diligent attention to program management and evaluation. The board finds that the operation of the NRI grant program has been enhanced; however, more can be done.

The board recommends that the NRI program managers pursue additional opportunities for improvement in making more systematic evaluations of program performance, redoubling efforts to promote multidisciplinary research, and continuing to assure the relevance of the NRI grant agenda to national goals.

Although work on such initiatives must be ongoing, particular attention should be paid to enhancing the visibility of the competitive grants program now, on the threshold of what the board hopes will be significant expansion for the NRI.

Evaluation

In its 1989 report, the board recognized the particular need for evaluation of a new program that had unusual features: a strong emphasis on multidisciplinary grants, a new type of mission-linked team grant, research-strengthening grants, and an extremely broad programmatic scope. Unfortunately, with growth in the NRI funding less than had been hoped and consequent efforts to hold down administrative costs, the NRI management has had only limited resources to devote to program evaluation. The board emphasizes that evaluation will not only improve the performance of the NRI but also provide evidence of the contributions it makes to national goals for competitiveness, human health, and the environment.

The board believes that the NRI should initiate a vigorous effort to define key performance measures for the program, including the participation of the broader science community and the effectiveness of the variety of grant types, especially multidisciplinary. Further, systematic documentation of the program's scientific and socioeconomic benefits should be pursued. USDA's Economic Research Service should be enlisted to cooperate with NRI scientists in an effort to translate benefits into socioeconomic terms. The lack of an accepted methodology for research program evaluation is not peculiar to the NRI. However, the NRI could provide leadership in the effort to design assessments of research that help establish accountability in the use of public funds. The White House statement on science policy emphasized the need "to put in place better mechanisms to evaluate our investment strategy" and directed each federal science agency to "develop measures to evaluate its contributions" (Executive Office of the President, Office of Science and Technology Policy, 1994). Evaluation across the four funding mechanisms—competitive grants, formula funds, special grants, and intramural research—would be appropriate as well.

Life scientists, engineers, and social scientists might collaborate in devising methods for evaluating the NRI's contributions to the advancement of science and to broad socioeconomic goals. Although assessment of the output of basic research is notoriously difficult, there are measures that might provide some information. Numbers of patents generated might be one such indicator, for example, although the temptation to err on the side of being too mechanistic has to be resisted. The methodology of evaluation should be established clearly so that the data the methodology requires can be collected during the research project and so that other appropriate information, for example, the impact on industry or consumers, can be identified and gathered.

Multidisciplinary Research

The board had hoped that the NRI would provide significant new opportunities for multidisciplinary research. Opportunities for work at the intersection of disciplines often lead to advances of fundamental importance. Multidisciplinary research projects are notoriously difficult to design and execute, however. The board commends the NRI program managers for recognizing these difficulties. Further consideration, however, should be given to offering planning grants to prospective research teams, extending the funding period for multidisciplinary grants to 4 years, and finding innovative ways to identify individual contributions to multidisciplinary team research projects. An increase in the funds available to the NRI would allow a balance of effort between fundamental and mission-linked multidisciplinary work. At the same time, the NRI should continue its attempts to avoid appearance of equating a program area with a specific discipline. Problems in animal systems, for example, may be jointly or separately addressed by animal scientists, engineers, human nutritionists, crop scientists, and economists. Refinements of the requests for grant proposals and in the selection of peer reviewers will expedite the integration of disciplines in every program area.

Relevancy

Finally, the board observes that scientific understanding of a food and fiber system contributes to and supports the goal of sustaining that system. Ultimately, it is a farming or forestry system, not an individual practice, that is judged to be sustainable or not. By the same reasoning, it is unwise to attempt to judge each grant proposal as a stand-alone proposition, out of context of the system in which it will ultimately find application. Moreover, it is difficult to find objective criteria on which to judge sustainability, a working definition of which continues to be hotly disputed.

Coordination

In carrying out the mandate to pursue research to support a sustainable food and fiber system, the board recommends that the USDA research managers continue to seek a better understanding of the relationship between individual research projects and attainment of national goals. However, the board believes that a single set of criteria derived from a legislative definition of sustainable agriculture will not provide adequate guidance in selection of projects to support.

Although advances in fundamental science may be critical to the development of new technologies, or even make them possible, it is usually difficult to make an a priori judgment about the value of that basic work, which is what use of a relevancy protocol might dictate. However, all can agree on the need to continue to search for a better way to evaluate the outcomes of agricultureal science. Effective evaluation holds promise for improving program management, but more important, it serves as a way to identify and perhaps reconcile differences over the ultimate goals of agricultural research.

References

Agricultural Outlook. 1994. Statistical indictors. (November):32-58.

Alston, J. M., P. G. Pardey, and H. O. Carter, eds. 1994. Valuing UC Agricultural Research and Extension. Publication. No. VR-1. Davis: Agricultural Issues Center, Division of Agriculture and Natural Resources, University of California.

Executive Office of the President, Office of Science and Technology Policy. 1994. Science in the National Interest. Washington, D.C.: U.S. Government Printing Office.

Center for Rural Affairs. 1991. Sustainable Agriculture in the National Research Initiative. Walthill, Neb.: Center for Rural Affairs.

Current Research Information System (CRIS). Beltsville, Md.: Cooperative Research Service, U.S. Department of Agriculture.

National Research Council. 1972. Report of the Committee on Research Advisory to the U.S. Department of Agriculture. Washington, D.C.: National Academy Press.

National Research Council. 1975. World Food and Nutrition Study: Enhancement of Food Production for the United States. Washington, D.C.: National Academy Press.

National Research Council. 1977. World Food and Nutrition Study: The Potential Contributions of Research. Washington, D.C.: National Academy Press.

National Research Council. 1989. Investing in Research: A Proposal to Strengthen the Agricultural, Food, and Environmental System. Washington, D.C.: National Academy Press.

National Research Council. 1993. Soil and Water Quality: An Agenda for Agriculture. Washington, D.C.: National Academy Press.

National Research Council. 1994a. The Funding of Young Investigators in the Biological and Biomedical Sciences. Washington, D.C.: National Academy Press.

National Research Council. 1994b. Rangeland Health: New Methods to Classify, Inventory, and Monitor Rangelands. Washington, D.C.: National Academy Press.

U.S. Department of Agriculture. 1993. Relevancy of AES Research to Sustainable Agriculture. April. Mimeograph.

APPENDIX

Executive Summary from *Investing in Research*

This is the technological age. It is also an age of opportunity. U.S. agriculture continuously evolves, but the pace of change is now more dramatic than ever. In the life sciences, new knowledge and instrumentation are rapidly expanding the understanding of plants, animals, and microbes; providing new opportunities to control disease and pests; and improving the quality of agricultural and food products. Equally complex changes are occurring in international trade, where the new rules of the global marketplace are transforming old patterns of competition.

In the agricultural system, as with other segments of U.S. industry, the problems of the twenty-first century intensify more quickly than ever before, and opportunities must be seized immediately, before their peak of potential benefit has passed. The ability of the United States to resolve the spectrum of issues and related problems in agriculture—nutrition, economics and international trade, production efficiency, natural resources conservation, control of pollutants, and others—depends on depth of knowledge, the available tools and technologies, and the skill and insight to apply them.

The United States needs to invest in the future—in human capital and the scientific knowledge base—to revitalize and reinvigorate one of its leading industries, the agricultural, food, and environmental system, in its broadest sense. A sound investment strategy for research is fundamental to sustain economic performance, to respond competitively to the increased economic strengths and manufacturing capacities of other nations, and to maintain the

U.S. quality of life. The commitment called for in this proposal should therefore be part of a national agenda to strengthen the United States.

URGENCY FOR CHANGE

Major challenges confronting the nation now center on the competitiveness of U.S. agricultural products in global trade, the safety and quality of the U.S. food supply, and the management and sustainability of the country's natural resources.

Competitiveness

The United States faces new and aggressive competition from abroad. The balance of trade has gone from positive to negative, making the United States a debtor nation. The strong role that agricultural exports played in the U.S. balance of payments has weakened. U.S. global competitiveness in agricultural commodities and food products has eroded because of increased costs of production at home and heightened competition from foreign producers in the marketplace. Given the high U.S. production capacity, regular surpluses of major commodities, and the imperative of deficit reduction, the needs for profitable new uses for agricultural products, more costefficient production, and new markets remain high.

Human Health and Well-Being

Nutritious and high-quality food is available to U.S. citizens. However, problems are arising that must be resolved, such as excessive fat in the diet, the incidence of microbial contamination, and pesticide residues on food.

U.S. citizens consume too many saturated fats. Although red meat and dairy products provide 36 percent of food energy and 100 percent of certain nutrients, they also contribute more than half of the total fat, nearly three-fourths of the saturated fatty acids, and all of the dietary cholesterol in the U.S. diet (National Research Council, 1988a). Agricultural research is focusing on ways to produce leaner animals and to process nutritious foods with reduced levels of saturated fats and cholesterol.

Salmonella species and *Campylobacter jejuni* from all sources are each responsible for up to 2,000 cases of gastroenteric disease per 100,000 people per year in the United States (National Research Council, 1985a). Illnesses caused by these microorganisms tend to be most severe among the very young, the very old, or patients with immunosuppressive diseases. New research can determine points at which known pathogens enter the food supply and can contribute to improving methods for detection, monitoring, and control.

Although potential cancer risks from ingesting pesticides in the diet are small in comparison with the potential risks from other known causes of cancer, the pesticide residues on fruits and vegetables are a growing public concern. Research can provide new insights into levels of dietary risk and can identify new alternatives that will ensure the producer a high-quality crop while reducing the need for pesticide application.

Natural Resources and the Environment

Concern for prudent natural resources stewardship and a clean and sustainable environment is now focusing on issues such as contamination of surface water and groundwater by natural and chemical fertilizers, pesticides, and sediment; the continued abuse of fragile and nutrient-poor soils; and suitable disposal of municipal, industrial, and agricultural wastes.

Water pollution is probably the most damaging and widespread environmental effect of agricultural production. Various estimates of the potential financial costs of surface water contamination from agricultural production are in excess of $2 billion per year. Groundwater is the source of public drinking water for nearly 75 million people. This fact is significant because accumulating evidence indicates that a growing number of contaminants from agricultural production are found in underground water supplies. Although research is being conducted in these areas, a major increase in support will be required to adequately investigate and apply new knowledge and technologies to curtail surface water and groundwater contamination.

Soil erosion remains a serious environmental problem in parts of the United States, even after 50 years of state and federal efforts to control it. New data indicate that the intensive tillage practices associated with continuous monoculture or short crop rotations may make soils more susceptible to erosion. New knowledge will provide improved ways to estimate erosion, decrease the displacement of soils by wind and water, and develop federal policies for conserving fragile lands.

Waste disposal facilities all over the United States are reaching their capacities to contain and decompose plant and animal residues, pesticides, food processing wastes, sewage, and industrial sludges. Research in the agricultural, food, and environmental sciences can help minimize the production of waste materials, develop technologies to increase recycling, and develop improved systems for ecologically safe waste disposal systems.

New Knowledge

Solving the problems of competitiveness, a high-quality food supply, and natural resources and the environment will require much more new knowledge than was required to solve previous problems. An example illustrates the point: genetically engineered biocontrol agents for pest management are now being designed on the basis of current knowledge, but it will likely take a 10-fold increase in understanding of the biology of such agents and their survival and action in various ecosystems before such engineered biological control agents can be effectively developed and used. The knowledge needed must come from a number of disciplines, such as biochemistry, genetics, physiology, plant pathology, entomology, plant biology, ecosystems analysis, agronomy, and economics, among others. The specific disciplinary knowledge must then be integrated into effective production systems. The knowledge required far transcends that necessary for the current chemical-based technologies.

The necessary new knowledge is unlikely to be acquired and expediently applied without substantial new funding.

This proposal for investment in research for the agricultural, food, and environmental system aims to establish the new knowledge base necessary to address the problems.

THE PROPOSAL

The purpose of this proposal—as well as the challenge it presents—is to mobilize the nation's scientific and engineering communities to advance the quality of agriculture, the food supply, and the environment.

This proposal presents a program to strengthen the focus of U.S. science on agriculture. The premise is that a judicious but substantial increase in research funding through competitive grants is the best way to sustain and strengthen the U.S. agricultural, food, and environmental system.

Implementation of this research proposal will

- Capture the proven high economic return on investment in agricultural research.
- Secure for agricultural research a full array of talent from the entire U.S. science and technology research sector.
- Expand knowledge in all the disciplines underpinning agriculture while also contributing to advances in other broad areas such as biomedicine, ecology, engineering, education, and economics.

This proposal, which is composed of the following specific elements, should be evaluated as a singular strategy for action.

An Expanded Public Investment

Research support for agriculture, food, and the environment should be increased by $500 million annually. This increase should support competitive grants administered through the U.S. Department of Agriculture's Competitive Research Grants Office.

Appendix

This competitive grants program should be increased to support the need for research in public and private universities and colleges; not-for-profit institutions; the U.S. Department of Agriculture's (USDA's) Agricultural Research Service, Economic Research Service, and U.S. Forest Service; and other research agencies of the state and federal governments.

Funds should come from new monies, not from the redirection or reallocation of existing research and education programs, including formula-funded programs.

Program Areas and Scientific Scope

The expanded proposed competitive grants program should encompass all science and technology relevant to research needs for agriculture, food, and the environment. To do this, six program areas should be established: (1) plant systems; (2) animal systems; (3) nutrition, food quality, and health; (4) natural resources and the environment; (5) engineering, products, and processes; and (6) markets, trade, and policy.

Agriculture has vastly overgrown its early bounds of planting and harvesting crops and nurturing livestock as sources of food and fiber. It is a major influence on and component of industry, world trade, and global ecology. The six program areas establish a framework that will accommodate all areas of research relating to agriculture, food, and the environment. Research in the six program areas using all relevant disciplines of science and technology is essential to solve current and emerging problems.

Examples of some of the major topics within the six program areas are as follows.

- *Plant Systems:* plant genome structure and function; molecular and cellular genetics and plant biotechnology; plant-pest interactions and biocontrol systems; crop plant response to environmental stresses; improved nutrient qualities of plant products; and new food and industrial uses of plant products.
- *Animal Systems:* cellular and molecular basis of animal reproduction, growth, disease, and health; identification of genes responsible for improved production traits and resistance to disease; improved nutritional performance of animals; and improved nutrient qualities of animal products.
- *Nutrition, Food Quality, and Health:* microbial contaminants and pesticide residues related to human health; links between diet and health; bioavailability of nutrients; postharvest physiology and practices; and improved processing technologies.

- *Natural Resources and the Environment:* fundamental structures and functions of ecosystems; biological and physical bases of sustainable production systems; minimizing soil and water losses and sustaining surface water and groundwater quality; global climatic effects on agriculture; forestry; and biological diversity.
- *Engineering, Products, and Processes:* new uses and new products from traditional crops, animals, by-products, and natural resources; robotics, energy efficiency, computing, and expert systems; new hazard and risk assessment and mitigation measures; and water quality and management.
- *Markets, Trade, and Policy:* optimal strategies for entering and being competitive in overseas markets; new decision tools for on-farm and in-market systems; choices and applications of technology; and new approaches to economic development and viability in the rural United States and developing nations.

Grant Types

In each of the six program areas, four types of competitive grants should be available: (1) principal investigator grants, (2) fundamental multidisciplinary team grants, (3) mission-linked multidisciplinary team grants, and (4) research-strengthening grants.

Principal investigator grants should support individual scientists or coinvestigators working within the same, or closely related, disciplines. Principal investigator grants are the foundation of the highly successful competitive grants programs in the United States, and they are the major way to attract and retain talented scientists and their students into areas of research.

Fundamental multidisciplinary team grants should support collaborating scientists from two or more disciplines focusing on basic science or engineering questions. It is often at the juncture of disciplines that new discoveries and research strategies are made.

Mission-linked multidisciplinary team grants should support multidisciplinary research focusing on more applied problems of national significance and should be linked to, among others, the Cooperative Extension Service (CES), the Agricultural Research Service (ARS), and industry. Funding through this grant type will facilitate the application of knowledge and the transfer of technology to the user through joint research-extension studies.

Research-strengthening grants should competitively support institutions through program grants and individuals through fellowships to increase the U.S. research capacity.

Attention to Multidisciplinary Research

The expanded competitive grants program should give major emphasis to supporting both fundamental and mission-linked multidisciplinary research teams. Up to 50 percent of the funding awarded for USDA's competitive grants should support multidisciplinary research.

The significance of multidisciplinary research to the success of the competitive grants program cannot be overemphasized. Many fundamental scientific and technological questions—and certainly the more applied problems—are multifaceted. To deal with their inherent complexity and diversity, it is necessary to establish multidisciplinary grants and make them a major feature of the expanded program.

Strengthening Institutions and Human Resources

Research-strengthening grants to institutions and individuals should be a key component of an expanded competitive grants program.

Research-strengthening grants are essential for two reasons. Grants to institutions improve the research capability at institutions and in departments that aspire to, but have not attained, nationally recognized research and development (R&D) capabilities. Fellowships increase the training and experiences available to pre- and postdoctoral fellows in agricultural, food, and environmental research. Expanding the number of women, underrepresented minorities, and disabled individuals in the research system must be integral to the entire program. The research-strengthening grant is a major way to provide those opportunities. The grants are not intended to be used for buildings or major capital expenditures.

Size and Duration of Support

The size and duration of USDA competitive grant awards should be increased substantially. The average size of a grant should be at least $100,000 per year per principal investigator; the duration of a grant should be at least 3 and as many as 5 years.

The size and duration of awards reflect the capability of a program to attract top-quality scientific and engineering talent. The USDA Competitive Research Grants Office should award grants that are adequate to conduct effective research and that are comparable in size and duration to those awarded by the National Science Foundation (NSF) and the National Institutes of

Health (NIH), the two institutions in the United States with the largest and most successful grants programs. The proposed changes in size and duration will attract more top scientists in a variety of disciplines and thus increase the capacity to educate their students—the nation's future scientists.

RATIONALE FOR THE PROPOSAL

Key parts to the rationale for the expanded program include the need for a federal initiative; the need for a large increase in funding; the justification for new money, not for the redirection of current funds; the suitability of USDA as the central agency for the expanded program; and the appropriateness of competitive grants as the funding mechanism.

A Federal Initiative

A federal initiative for increased research support is needed because the issues and fundamental research needs are national in scope, and the nation as a whole, not just a state or region, is the beneficiary. In addition, states lack the funding to advance basic science across the full range of areas requiring immediate attention. In the private sector, the rate of R&D growth, which has been strong since the mid-1970s, is likely to level off in the decade ahead, and it may decline somewhat. Moreover, private sector research is focused on creating opportunities to market products and services, whereas much of the research most important to society and the nation is not market-related.

A $500 Million Increase

A $500 million increase in research funding is justified for at least three major reasons. (1) The pervasive needs and problems require large amounts of new knowledge and technology for their resolution, as discussed earlier. (2) Agricultural research provides a high return on investment. (3) The agricultural research system, as presently funded, is unable to provide the necessary financial support for the quality, amount, and breadth of science and technology necessary to address the problems.

Agricultural research characteristically gives a high annual return on investment, more than 45 percent (Fox et al., 1987). The contributions of research conducted within the competitive grants program will, in addition, bring advances not only to agriculture, food, and the environment but also to other scientific disciplines and other sectors of society. Discoveries that were made in efforts to resolve agricultural problems have already led to major advances in biology and medicine. Findings from research with plant models, for example, will lead to advances in the understanding of basic genetics and gene expression. Over time, the research results and their application will significantly decrease both regulatory and environmental costs.

Adequate funding through the six proposed program areas must be available to support the best and brightest researchers currently working in agriculture and to attract top researchers in other disciplines who have not previously participated in USDA programs. Current funding cannot do either.

Researchers' proposals for scientific inquiry are currently funded at levels that are too low to meet the demands of high-quality science. The average annual grant size from USDA is $50,000, in contrast to average annual grant sizes of $71,300 from NSF and $154,900 from NIH. USDA grants average 2 years in contrast to 3 years or more for NSF and NIH. In addition to funding grants at a higher level, both NSF and NIH fund a much larger number of grants. In fiscal year 1988, USDA awarded approximately S40 million for competitive grants, in contrast to the $265 million awarded by the Directorate of Biological, Behavioral, and Social Sciences at NSF and the $632 million awarded by the National Institute for General Medical Sciences (NIGMS), which is only 1 of the 12 institutes of NIH. All of the institutes that make up the NIH together awarded $6.4 billion in competitive research grants in 1988. Research supported by NIGMS is broad, covering all areas of fundamental biomedical science that bridge the responsibilities of all the institutes within NIH. Research supported by the USDA's competitive grants program is narrow, covering only some of the six program areas recommended in this proposal.

The proposed increase of $500 million would expand the current competitive grants program level of $50 million to an annual total of at least $550 million. The overall $550 million program should support the following four types of grants:

1. About 800 principal investigator grants for an average duration of 3 years. Total annual expenditure: $250 million.
2. bout 180 fundamental multidisciplinary team grants for an average duration of 4 years. Total annual expenditure: $150 million.
3. About 60 mission-linked multidisciplinary team grants for an average duration of 4 years. Total annual expenditure: $100 million.
4. Research-strengthening grants to institutions for programs and to individuals for fellowships. Total annual expenditure: $50 million.

The expansion of USDA's competitive grants program by $500 million from its current level of $50 million will enable USDA to significantly support the innovative science that is poised to proceed—as soon as funding can be obtained.

Support with New Money

Support of the competitive grants program with new money will reverse the consequences of no R&D growth in agriculture and sustain the state-federal partnership.

The publicly funded research system has not been able to investigate many scientific questions comprehensively because fiscal constraints have allowed little, if any, real growth in R&D expenditures. From 1955 through 1988, research funding for USDA remained virtually stable in constant dollars, corrected for inflation. The purchasing power actually decreased, and higher costs are associated with the potent but costly instruments and supplies required by today's researchers. In 1988 USDA's total annual R&D funding was only 4.6 percent of the total R&D funded by the federal government, exclusive of the Department of Defense. Unfortunately, the lack of growth in USDA's support for R&D from 1955 through 1988 did not allow sufficient advancement in scientific knowledge. The agricultural sector cannot progress under the current level of funding; it can only fall behind.

The lack of real growth in R&D expenditures during the past 30 years has slowed research within U.S. agriculture and other areas of science. Opportunities are missed, such as the relatively slow application of biotechnology to agricultural issues; problems have increased, such as the need for new uses for commodity crops and for improved new crops for better nutrient composition and postharvest quality. At the same time, however, science and technology in other countries are advancing rapidly. Without a new infusion of funds, there will be insufficient support for the talented researchers with new ideas that can refuel scientific advancement in U.S. agriculture. Furthermore, without new funding, prospective students and new Ph.D. graduates will not be attracted to careers in agriculture or retained in them.

Most states support research at land-grant universities and state agricultural experiment stations (SAESs) far in excess of the matching formula funds they receive from the federal government. A substantial portion of this state support goes to research on fundamental scientific problems of national importance. Increased federal support for competitive grants will ease that burden and allow more of the state funds to be used for problems specific to that state or region.

Redirection of funds from intramural or formula-based programs to competitive grants would be counter-productive. The delivery system—SAES scientists and extension specialists and advisers, in combination with government and the private sector—is already unduly stressed, and redirection would exacerbate staffing insufficiencies for ARS, CES, and SAESs.

Appendix

The Central Role of USDA

USDA is the federal agency responsible for advancing the agricultural sciences and developing technology applicable to food, fiber, and forest product industries. It is the entity best suited to administer the agricultural, food, and environmental competitive grants program.

The competitive grants program will warrant status as an independent office within USDA's Office of Science and Education, setting its administrator on a par with the administrators of the Agricultural Research Service, Cooperative State Research Service, and Extension Service as the managers of USDA's science, education, and training activities. As the USDA competitive grants program grows from about $50 million to $550 million in annual awards, changes in administrative procedures and institutional relationships will be essential.

Competitive Grants

The competitive grant is the proven and appropriate mechanism to stimulate new research in high-priority areas of science and engineering. It is flexible, reaches a large pool of talented scientists, and provides a balance to the overall research program, thereby ensuring high-quality research.

Responsiveness and flexibility in altering the direction of exploratory research are critical to scientific excellence. A competitive grants program capitalizes on the skills and experiences of leading scientists in recognizing the need for new directions in science. Because funding commitments to any one project are for only 3 to 5 years, this mechanism is flexible and responsive to rapid advancements in science, thereby allowing resources to be targeted at the most promising areas of scientific research in each grant cycle.

Sufficient funding over an adequate period of time is the best way to attract talented scientists from a variety of disciplines. The expanded competitive grants program will more adequately support researchers within the agricultural research system and will also open the system to scientists from other disciplines who have not previously participated in the USDA grants program. These scientists should be, but are not now, applying their skills to agricultural research.

An expanded competitive grants program will provide the needed balance among the funding mechanisms that support USDA R&D: intramural programs, formula funding, special grants, and competitive grants. Competitive grants are a significant source of funding within other federal agencies. At NIH and NSF, 83 and 90 percent of R&D support, respectively, is distributed through competitive research grants. At USDA, however, less than 6 percent of R&D support is so distributed. USDA should not attempt to mirror NIH and NSF in the proportion of funds it distributes on a competitive basis. Problems specific to certain crops, technologies, and regions are often best addressed through formula funds or special grants. Long-range research, such as the development of improved plant and animal germplasms, or tracking of the diets and nutritional status of a group of children as they grow, for example, are more effectively supported on a continuing basis through intramural funding. With full funding of this proposal, the annual investment in R&D by USDA would rise to $1.54 billion from $1.04 billion (Office of Management and Budget, 1989), and the $550 million in competitive grants would then account for approximately 35 percent of USDA's research expenditures.

FISCAL REALITIES

The recommendation for a major increase in funding of competitive research grants for agricultural, food, and environmental research comes at a time of overall fiscal constraint for the nation. Elected and public officials must reduce the national debt and at the same time set priorities among competing federal expenditures to enact programs that maintain the welfare, infrastructure, security, and continued economic growth of the United States. As a part of that they must also address public concerns for maintaining global competitiveness, the safety and nutritional quality of the food supply, and environmental resources. The goal of reducing expenditures while allocating funds for essential programs thus requires fiscal prudence.

Trade-Offs

Political leaders will need to consider the proposal for an increased commitment to agricultural, food, and environmental research against a background of potential trade-offs. What are these trade-offs?

- The additional $500 million could come from sacrificing other USDA research programs. Can some current research programs be discontinued in an effort to strengthen competitive grants research?
- The necessary funds could be directed to research from other USDA budget categories. Commodity price supports, for example, have decreased from $26 billion to $11 billion during the past 3 years, as U.S. agricultural export prices have improved. Should $500 million of those savings and future budgetary savings be redirected toward research, toward reducing the national debt, toward a combination of the two, or toward progress outside of agriculture?
- The funds could be shifted from other parts of the federal budget into USDA. Does the consistently high return on the agricultural research investment override the need for funds in other areas of national interest?

Appendix 57

- The investment in agricultural, food, and environmental research can be deferred until deficit reduction has been achieved. But investing new funds now can hasten future economic and scientific benefits. What will be gained—or lost—by postponing the investment?

Redirection within the USDA Research Budget

For the past 25 years the USDA budget for research has not increased. Actual monetary increases have barely kept up with inflation. In 1965 the USDA research budget had the purchasing power of $788 million in 1982 dollars; the 1988 research budget was valued at $778 million in 1982 dollars. In reality, any past changes in agricultural research priorities had to come from the redirection of funds within the research budget. Further redirection by increasing the investment in competitively awarded grants does not address the problem of the continued federal underinvestment in research through USDA. It also raises the real risk of destroying some of the "muscle" of current high-quality research in intramural and formula-funded research in attempts to cut out any "fat."

Without some real growth in the USDA research budget, there can be no realistic opportunity to broaden the scope of science contributing to agricultural, food, and environmental research. Many of the new scientific opportunities that require costly supplies and instrumentation will have to remain unexplored, and few multidisciplinary research teams will be able to be formed to attack the multifaceted problems of competitiveness, food quality, and natural resources confronting agriculture.

The proposed increase in funding for competitive research grants is justified. This proposal stands strongly against reallocation within the USDA research budget for the reasons given above. If no growth in the USDA research budget is possible, then decisions to redirect funds are judgments that elected and other public officials may choose to consider.

Reinvesting Subsidy Savings

As U.S. agriculture gradually returns to a state of economic health and as commodity prices return to free-market conditions, the federal budget appropriations currently used for price support programs may be targeted for budgetary savings. Part of these savings should be reinvested in research programs to strengthen the knowledge that supports the nation's food and fiber industries.

Federal Investment

Investments in agricultural research in the United States have consistently shown high returns, as noted previously. Such data demonstrate that an increased investment in the agricultural, food, and environmental research system will be paid back rapidly in economic development and other public benefits.

The U.S. gross national product in 1987 was $4.5 trillion (Council of Economic Advisers, 1989). Of that, the agribusiness complex contributed approximately 18 percent, or roughly $815 billion (Harrington et al., 1986). The current annual federal investment in agricultural R&D is about $1.04 billion—less than 0.13 percent of agriculture's annual contribution to the gross national product.

Investing Now

A major increase in research funding of $500 million is needed at this time. The scientific opportunities exist today to use this increased funding wisely. The needed scientific talent is available now, primarily through the nation's existing scientists in the physical, biological, engineering, and social sciences, as well as those in agriculture and related disciplines, who are ready to compete for this new funding. In addition, as noted above, increased funding will also ensure the flow of young scientists into agriculture-related research areas.

To achieve the maximum effect, this substantial increase should be enacted in a single year as a reflection of the value of the broadened scope of agricultural, food, and environmental research and the importance of the sustained advancement of this system to the U.S. economy.

Given the overall fiscal problems facing the nation, the appropriation of the full $500 million increase may not be possible in a single year. Even so, a commitment of this magnitude is essential. Any stepwise increase in funding should provide the full increase as soon as possible, preferably within 3 years, and be balanced to address the needs and opportunities in agriculture, food, and the environment.

CONCLUSION

Agriculture is the world's oldest and largest industry, and it has been a highly successful industry in the United States. The United States is endowed with perhaps the world's most extensive and abundant complement of soils, water, and climate favorable for agricultural production. Still, several other countries have tremendous natural assets to draw upon in developing productive agricultural industries. One dominant factor stands out in making possible the remarkable pace of development of agriculture in this country in contrast to that in other countries—the early and very strong support given to agriculture by the U.S. government. Agriculture was the first—and for a long time, the major—federally supported scientific effort. It is significant that early federal support was not directed primarily toward infrastructure investments that yielded only quick benefits. Rather, support was broad, and a large proportion was directed toward research and education.

The decision to provide federal support for a strong U.S. agricultural system was made by the Congress 127 years ago through the Morrill Act of 1862. Now is the time to make a renewed investment in U.S. agriculture, one that will ensure its worldwide leadership role in the coming decades.

As a leader, the United States calls upon its agricultural and food system to compete in a free-market world. But U.S. farmers cannot compete with the price of labor in many countries, where it is far lower than that in the United States. And, for the same reason, they cannot compete with the cost of fertile land in other countries. The single resource that U.S. farmers can draw upon to capture the leading edge is science and technology. The U.S. government must help to provide an environment where U.S. producers and processors can compete. The most effective way to ensure a strong U.S. agricultural system is to capitalize on science and technology by investing strongly in agricultural, food, and environmental research.

APPENDIX REFERENCES

Council of Economic Advisers. 1989. Economic Report of the President. Washington, D.C.: U.S. Government Printing Office.

Fox, G., R. Evenson, and V. Ruttan. 1987. Balancing basic and applied science: The case for agricultural research. Bioscience 37:507-509.

Harrington, D., G. Schluter, and P. O'Brien. 1986. Agriculture's Links to the National Economy. Economic Research Service, Agriculture Information Bulletin No. 504. Washington, D.C.: U.S. Department of Agriculture.

National Research Council. 1985. Meat and Poultry Inspection: The Scientific Basis of the Nation's Program. Washington, D.C.: National Academy Press.

National Research Council. 1988. Designing Foods: Animal Product Options in the Marketplace. Washington, D.C.: National Academy Press.

Office of Management and Budget. 1989. Budget of the United States Government. Special Analysis J. Washington, D.C.: U.S. Government Printing Office.

About the Authors

Dale E. Bauman (*chairman*) is professor of nutritional biochemistry in the Department of Animal Science at Cornell University. He received his undergraduate and masters' degrees from Michigan State University and his Ph.D. in nutrition-biochemistry from the University of Illinois. Prior to his appointment at Cornell University, he was a faculty member of the Department of Dairy Science at the University of Illinois. His research areas include regulation of nutrient use in bovine lactation, growth, and pregnancy and bovine mammary gland biology. Bauman and his colleagues crystallized the concept of homeorhesis, the process of long-term regulation of nutrient use during a particular physiological state such as lactation. He has been a member of the National Academy of Sciences since 1988.

Philip H. Abelson was, from 1962 to 1984, the editor of *Science* and since 1984 has been *Science*'s deputy editor for science and engineering. Abelson has B.S. and M.S. degrees from Washington State University and a Ph.D. degree in nuclear physics from the University of California at Berkeley. He was affiliated with the Carnegie Institution of Washington, Stanford, California, from 1946 to 1978. Among his principal scientific achievements, he was the first American to identify products of uranium fission (1939); co-discovered, with E. M. McMillan, neptunium (1940); developed the liquid thermal diffusion process to separate uranium isotopes (1942-1944); and produced a series of studies on the fate of organic chemicals in geological settings leading to petroleum and natural gas formulations (1960-1970). He was elected to the National Academy of Sciences in 1959.

John M. Antle is a professor in the Department of Agricultural Economics and Economics at Montana State University. His research areas and teaching fields include environmental and natural resource issues in agriculture, econometric analysis of agricultural production, international economics, and economic development. He joined the university as an associate professor in 1987. From 1989 to 1990 he served as a senior economist on the President's Council of Economic Advisers, where he was responsible for agricultural, trade, and environmental policy. He received his B.S. degree at Albion College and his M.S. and Ph.D. degrees in economics from the University of Chicago.

William B. Delauder became the eighth president of Delaware State University in 1987. Prior to assuming this post, he served as dean of the College of Arts and Sciences at North Carolina Agricultural and Technical State University. His B.S. degree is from Morgan State College and his Ph.D. degree in physical chemistry from Wayne State University. He conducted research in physical biochemistry at the Centre de Biophysique Moleculaire du C.N.R.S. in France as a postdoctoral fellow from 1969 to 1971. His research on the physical properties of macromolecular systems and on the fluorescence properties of proteins has been published in leading scientific journals. In 1990 he was appointed to the National Advisory Council of the National Institute of General Medical Sciences of the National Institutes of Health.

Susan K. Harlander is the director of dairy foods research and development at Land O'Lakes, Inc., Minneapolis, Minnesota. She holds an M.S. degree in microbiology and a Ph.D. degree in food science from the University of Minnesota. Harlander was on the faculty at the University of Minnesota from 1985 to 1992 when she left to join Land O'Lakes, Inc. Harlander initiated and coordinated the First International Symposium on Biotechnology in the Food Processing Industry in 1985. In Washington, she serves as a member of the Science and Education Advisory Committee (1992-1994) and the Agricultural Biotechnology Research Advisory Committee (1992-1994) for the U.S. Department of Agriculture.

Richard R. Harwood has held the C. S. Mott Foundation Chair of Sustainable Agriculture at Michigan State University's Department of Crop and Soil Sciences since 1990. From 1985 to 1990 he was director of the Asian Program for Winrock International, Morrilton, Arkansas. Major accomplishments include conceptualizing and implementing the International Rice Research Institute's cropping systems program, which focused on farmer-collaborative research, and developing research methodologies including the "land equivalent ratio" for evaluating intercrop systems. He received his M.Sc. and his Ph.D. degrees in plant breeding from Michigan State University. His areas of expertise include small-farm agricultural systems in the humid tropics and methods for biological integration of agronomic systems.

T. Kent Kirk is director of the Institute for Microbial and Biochemical Technology of the Forest Products Laboratory (FPL), Forest Service, U.S. Department of Agriculture (USDA), in Madison, Wisconsin; USDA professor in the Department of Bacteriology, University of Wisconsin-Madison, and adjunct professor in the Department of Wood and Paper Science, North Carolina State University. Kirk's current research includes the biochemistry and physiology of wood decomposition by fungi and the industrial application of fungi and enzymes. Kirk's B.S. degree in forestry is. from Louisiana Polytechnic Institute; M.S. and Ph.D. (biochemistry and plant pathology) degrees are from North Carolina State University. In 1988, Kirk was elected to the National Academy of Sciences.

James R. Moseley is director of agricultural services and regulations at Purdue University and is Indiana's lead administrative authority for agricultural and regulatory functions located at Purdue University and for other organizations and programs that impact on the jurisdiction of this office. Moseley served for 2 years as assistant secretary of agriculture for natural resources and the environment, directing policies and supervising activities and programs of the U.S. Forest Service and the U.S. Soil Conservation Service. He also served as adviser to the U.S. Environmental Protection Agency (1989-1990) concerning environmental issues directly affecting the agricultural industry. Moseley received a B.S. degree in horticulture from Purdue University. After graduation he began a farming operation that is now a grain and hog enterprise.

Norman R. Scott is vice president for research and advanced studies at Cornell University, responsible for the coordination of all research, including the oversight of patents, technology marketing, grants, and contracts. He received a B.S.A.E. degree with honors from Washington State University and a Ph.D. degree from Cornell University. He has been a member of the Cornell faculty since 1962 in the Department of Agricultural and Biological Engineering. Recent projects have included electronic applications in agriculture. Scott was elected technical vice-president of the American Society of Agricultural Engineers in 1989 for a 3-year term and is currently president (1993-1994). He was elected to the National Academy of Engineering in 1990.

George E. Seidel, Jr., is a professor of physiology at Colorado State University. He joined the Department of Physiology in 1971 as assistant professor. From 1986 to 1987, he was a visiting scientist at the Whitehead Institute working in molecular biology; from 1978 to 1979 he was visiting associate professor in the Biology Department at Yale University working in developmental biology. Before joining the faculty of Colorado State University, he was trained, as a research fellow, in electron microscopy in the Anatomy Department at Harvard Medical School (1970-1971). His B.S. degree is from The Pennsylvania State University and his M.S. and Ph.D. degrees in reproductive physiology are from Cornell University. Seidel was elected to the National Academy of Sciences in 1992.

Christopher R. Somerville is the director of the Department of Plant Biology of the Carnegie Institution of Washington in Stanford, California, and a professor in the Department of Biological Sciences at Stanford University. From 1982 until 1993 he was a faculty member in the Department of Botany and Plant Pathology and Michigan State University-Department of Energy Plant Research Laboratory. He earned his M.Sc. and his Ph.D. in genetics from the University of Alberta. His primary area of research is physiological genetics and biochemistry of lipid metabolism and membrane biogenesis in higher plants and molecular genetics of Arabidopsis. He was elected a fellow of the Royal Society of London in 1991.

Patricia B. Swan is vice provost for research and advanced studies and dean of the graduate college at Iowa State University (ISU) with administrative oversight of all graduate and research programs and technology transfer programs. She served as the U.S. Department of Agriculture's nutrition program coordinator for science and education (1979 to 1980) and program manager for competitive grants (1985 to 1986). Swan's research interests include nutrient metabolism, animal models for human genetic disease, and the history of research on nutritional biochemistry in the United States. Her B.S. degree is from the University of North Carolina at Greensboro and M.S. (nutrition) and Ph.D. (biochemistry and nutrition) degrees are from the University of Wisconsin-Madison.

John R. Welser is vice president of the Agricultural and Pharmaceutical Research Divisions, and vice president of Animal Health Research and Biologics, for The Upjohn Company, Kalamazoo, Michigan. He has served on the faculties of Purdue University (1964 to 1970) and the University of Georgia (1970 to 1975). In 1975, he became the dean of the College of Veterinary Medicine at Michigan State University and served in that capacity until 1983 when he joined The Upjohn Company. Welser received B.S., D.V.M., and M.S. (surgery and medicine) degrees from Michigan State University and a Ph.D. degree (veterinary anatomy and endocrinology) from Purdue University.

Recent Publications of the Board on Agriculture

Policy and Resources

Rangeland Health: New Methods to Classify, Inventory, and Monitor Rangelands (1994), 180 pp., ISBN 0-309-04879-6

Soil and Water Quality: An Agenda for Agriculture (1993), 516 pp., ISBN 0-309-04933-4

Managing Global Genetic Resources: Agricultural Crop Issues and Policies (1993), 450 pp., ISBN 0-309-04430-8

Pesticides in the Diets of Infants and Children (1993), 408 pp., ISBN 0-309-04875-3

Managing Global Genetic Resources: Livestock (1993), 294 pp., ISBN 0-309-04394-8

Sustainable Agriculture and the Environment in the Humid Tropics (1993), 720 pp., ISBN 0-309-04749-8

Agriculture and the Undergraduate: Proceedings (1992), 296 pp., ISBN 0-309-04682-3

Water Transfers in the West: Efficiency, Equity, and the Environment (1992), 320 pp., ISBN 0-309-04528-2

Managing Global Genetic Resources: Forest Trees (1991), 244 pp., ISBN 0-309-04034-5

Managing Global Genetic Resources: The U.S. National Plant Germplasm System (1991), 198 pp., ISBN 0-309-04390-5

Sustainable Agriculture Research and Education in the Field: A Proceedings (1991), 448 pp., ISBN 0-309-04578-9

Toward Sustainability: A Plan for Collaborative Research on Agriculture and Natural Resource Management (1991), 164 pp., ISBN 0-309-04540-1

Investing in Research: A Proposal to Strengthen the Agricultural, Food, and Environmental System (1989), 156 pp., ISBN 0-309-04127-9

Alternative Agriculture (1989), 464 pp., ISBN 0-309-03985-1

Understanding Agriculture: New Directions for Education (1988), 80 pp., ISBN 0-309-03936-3

Designing Foods: Animal Product Options in the Marketplace (1988), 394 pp., ISBN 0-309-03798-0; ISBN 0-309-03795-6 (pbk)

Agricultural Biotechnology: Strategies for National Competitiveness (1987), 224 pp., ISBN 0-309-03745-X

Regulating Pesticides in Food: The Delaney Paradox (1987), 288 pp., ISBN 0-309-03746-8

Pesticide Resistance: Strategies and Tactics for Management (1986), 480 pp., ISBN 0-309-03627-5

Pesticides and Groundwater Quality: Issues and Problems in Four States (1986), 136 pp., ISBN 0-309-03676-3

Soil Conservation: Assessing the National Resources Inventory, Volume 1 (1986), 134 pp., ISBN 0-309-03649-9; Volume 2 (1986), 314 pp., ISBN 0-309-03675-5

New Directions for Biosciences Research in Agriculture: High-Reward Opportunities (1985), 122 pp., ISBN 0-309-03542-2

Genetic Engineering of Plants: Agricultural Research Opportunities and Policy Concerns (1984), 96 pp., ISBN 0-309-03434-5

Nutrient Requirements of Domestic Animals Series and Related Titles

Metabolic Modifiers: Effects on the Nutrient Requirements of Food-Producing Animals (1994), 81 pp., ISBN 04997-0

Nutrient Requirements of Poultry, Ninth Revised Edition (1994), ISBN 0-309-04892-3

Nutrient Requirements of Fish (1993), 108 pp., ISBN 0-309-04891-5

Nutrient Requirements of Horses, Fifth Revised Edition (1989), 128 pp., ISBN 0-309-03989-4; diskette included

Nutrient Requirements of Dairy Cattle, Sixth Revised Edition, Update 1989 (1989), 168 pp., ISBN 0-309-03826-X; diskette included

Nutrient Requirements of Swine, Ninth Revised Edition (1988), 96 pp., ISBN 0-309-03779-4

Vitamin Tolerance of Animals (1987), 105 pp., ISBN 0-309-03728-X

Predicting Feed Intake of Food-Producing Animals (1986), 95 pp., ISBN 0-309-03695-X

Nutrient Requirements of Cats, Revised Edition (1986), 87 pp., ISBN 0-309-03682-8

Nutrient Requirements of Dogs, Revised Edition (1985), 79 pp., ISBN 0-309-03496-5

Nutrient Requirements of Sheep, Sixth Revised Edition (1985), 106 pp., ISBN 0-309-03596-1

Nutrient Requirements of Beef Cattle, Sixth Revised Edition (1984), 90 pp., ISBN 0-309-03447-7

Further information, additional titles (prior to 1984), and prices are available from the National Academy Press, 2101 Constitution Avenue, NW, Washington, DC 20418, 202/334-3313 (information only); 800/624-6242 (orders only); 202/334-2451 (fax).